# Kitchen & Bath Drawing

Documents ◆ Drafting ◆ Presentation

**David Newton, CMKBD**
with Kelly Hayes

*Professional Resource Library*

# About The National Kitchen & Bath Association

As the only non-profit trade association dedicated exclusively to the kitchen and bath industry, the National Kitchen & Bath Association (NKBA) is the leading source of information and education for all professionals in the field.

NKBA's mission is to enhance member success and excellence by promoting professionalism and ethical business practices, and by providing leadership and direction for the kitchen and bath industry.

A non-profit trade association with more than 25,000 members in North America and overseas, it has provided valuable resources for industry professionals for more than forty years. Its members are the finest professionals in the kitchen and bath industry.

NKBA has pioneered innovative industry research, developed effective business management tools, and set groundbreaking standards for safe, functional and comfortable design of kitchens and baths.

NKBA provides a unique, one-stop resource for professional reference materials, seminars and workshops, distance learning opportunities, marketing assistance, design competitions, consumer referrals, job and internship opportunities and opportunities for volunteer leadership activities.

Recognized as the kitchen and bath industry's education and information leader, NKBA provides development opportunities and continuing education for all levels of professionals. More than 100 courses, as well as a certification program with three internationally recognized levels, help kitchen and bath professionals raise the bar for excellence.

For students entering the industry, NKBA offers Supported and Endorsed Programs, which provide NKBA-approved curriculum at more than 47 learning institutions throughout North America.

NKBA helps members and other industry professionals stay on the cutting-edge of an ever-changing field through the Association's Kitchen/Bath Industry Show, one of the largest trade shows in the country.

NKBA offers membership in four different categories: Industry, Associate, Student and Honorary. Industry memberships are broken into eleven different industry segments. For more information, visit NKBA at www.nkba.org.

# THANK YOU TO OUR SPONSORS

The National Kitchen & Bath Association recognizes with gratitude the following companies who generously helped to fund the creation of this industry resource.

**PATRONS**

www.americanwoodmark.com

www.kohler.com

## BENEFACTORS

www.monogram.com

www.subzero.com            www.wolfappliance.com

## CONTRIBUTOR

www.groheamerica.com

## SUPPORTERS

www.nyloft.net

www.showhouse.moen.com

# TOTO®

www.totousa.com

## DONORS

Rev-A-Shelf | Viking Range Corp. | Whirlpool Corp.

This book is intended for professional use by residential kitchen and bath designers. The procedures and advice herein have been shown to be appropriate for the applications described; however, no warranty (expressed or implied) is intended or given. Moreover, the user of this book is cautioned to be familiar with and to adhere to all manufacturers' planning, installation and use/care instructions. In addition, the user is urged to become familiar with and adhere to all applicable local, state and federal building codes, licensing and legislation requirements governing the user's ability to perform all tasks associated with design and installation standards, and to collaborate with licensed practitioners who offer professional services in the technical areas of mechanical, electrical and load bearing design as required for regulatory approval, as well as health and safety regulations.

Information about this book and other association programs
and publications may be obtained from the
National Kitchen & Bath Association
687 Willow Grove Street, Hackettstown, New Jersey 07840
Phone (800) 843-6522
www.nkba.org

ISBN 1-887127-59-3

First Edition 2006

Drawings and Illustrations: Jessica Best, Nicole Daniels
Jim Grinestaff, Bridget Miller and David Newton

Cover photos: Larry A. Falke Photography—Lake Forest, CA
Special thanks to Room Scapes—Laguna Niguel, CA

Published on behalf of NKBA by Fry Communications, Irvine, CA

Peer Reviewers

Timothy Aden, CMKBD

Julia Beamish, Ph.D, CKE

Leonard V. Casey

Ellen Cheever, CMKBD, ASID

Hank Darlington

Dee David, CKD, CBD

Peggy Deras, CKD, CID

Kimball Derrick, CKD

Tim DiGuardi

Kathleen Donohue, CMKBD

Gretchen L. Edwards, CMKBD

JoAnn Emmel, Ph.D

Jerry Germer

Pietro A. Giorgi, Sr., CMKBD

Tom Giorgi

Jerome Hankins, CKD

Spencer Hinkle, CKD

Max Isley, CMKBD

Mark Karas, CMKBD

Martha Kerr, CMKBD

Jim Krengel, CMKBD

Chris LaSpada, CPA

Elaine Lockard

Phyllis Markussen, Ed.D, CKE, CBE

Chris J Murphy, CKD, CBD, CKBI

David Newton, CMKBD

Roberta Null, Ph.D

Michael J Palkowitsch, CMKBD

Paul Pankow, CKBI, MA

Jack Parks

Kathleen R. Parrott, Ph.D, CKE

Al Pattison,CMKBD

Les Petrie, CMKBD

Becky Sue Rajala, CKD

Betty L. Ravnik, CKD, CBD

Robert Schaefer

Klaudia Spivey, CMKBD

Kelly Stewart, CMKBD

Tom Trzcinski, CMKBD

Stephanie Witt, CMKBD

# INTRODUCTION

Project documents, plans and drawings form the basis of communication within the kitchen and bath profession, and throughout the building industry as well. They detail the designer's vision of a project and are, in a sense, a specialized language through which a myriad of details are communicated to everyone involved in a job.

A set of kitchen and bath documents will be presented to your homeowner clients. They will guide the work of trades people such as electricians, plumbers, carpenters and contractors. Suppliers, including countertop fabricators and cabinet vendors, will rely on them to fulfill your order. And on large jobs, they may communicate your vision to allied professionals such as architects, interior designers and builders.

Properly prepared documents minimize costly and time-consuming errors during ordering and installation. Plus, they help clients visualize and understand their project upfront, avoiding misunderstandings later on.

Kitchen and bath project documents fulfill other roles, too. In some instances, they have legal implications. And they become part of your personal portfolio or resume, showcasing your work.

For all these reasons, the successful kitchen and bathroom designer should have the ability to produce a comprehensive and professional set of project documents. You present a professional image, not only to your clients and prospects, but also to other trades people, allied professionals, and even future employers, when you provide a set of project documents that everyone can clearly understand and use.

This book describes the most common project documents used in the kitchen and bath industry today, tells you how to prepare them, offers suggestions on presenting your designs, and includes the National Kitchen & Bath Association's Graphics and Presentation Standards (in Chapter 7) to guide your practice.

# Chapter 1: The Project Documents: Introduction of the Drawings and Forms

## THE SET OF DOCUMENTS

Kitchen and bath drawings, also referred to as plans, actually constitute a set of documents made up of many pages. Each document within the set is numbered and ordered, and cross referenced with other relevant documents.

Each sheet in a set of drawings is identified with a title block, usually at the bottom or side of the page. It pertains to the entire set of drawings and links each individual drawing sheet together as part of a total presentation.

Together they communicate the entire scope of the project, as well as all the pertinent details, so it is important that the entire set of documents, not just one individual drawing, be reviewed by everyone involved.

The words "plan," "drawing," "detail" and "blueprint" all refer to the illustrations for the project. A drawing can refer to any of the pages of the set. A blueprint is a copy of any drawing and can be blue or sienna in color.

The set of project documents typically is made up of at least a floor plan, a construction plan, a mechanical plan and elevations. There can also be a title page. Sometimes the set may include section drawings such as a countertop plan or a soffit plan. There may be additional interpretive drawings such as perspectives. The set of project documents can also include a schedule, specifications and perhaps a design statement.

Each element in a set of project documents is described here. You will learn how to create the various drawings as you read through this book. It is recommended that you read the entire book first, then return to the chapters that have step-by-step instructions for drafting and presentation.

**Figure 1.1** The title block on each sheet links together all the drawings in a set.

ALL DIMENSIONS AND SIZE DESIGNATIONS GIVEN ARE SUBJECT TO VERIFICATION ON JOB SITE AND ADJUSTMENT TO FIT JOB CONDITIONS.

NKBA — *The Finest Professionals in the Kitchen & Bath Industry* — National Kitchen & Bath Association

DESIGN PLANS ARE PROVIDED FOR THE FAIR USE BY THE CLIENT OR HIS AGENT IN COMPLETING THE PROJECT AS LISTED WITHIN THIS CONTRACT. DESIGN PLANS REMAIN THE PROPERTY OF THIS FIRM AND CAN NOT BE USED OR REUSED WITHOUT PERMISSION.

DESIGNED FOR: | BY: | DRWN | REV | DATE | BY | SCALE ½"=1'0" | DWG NO.

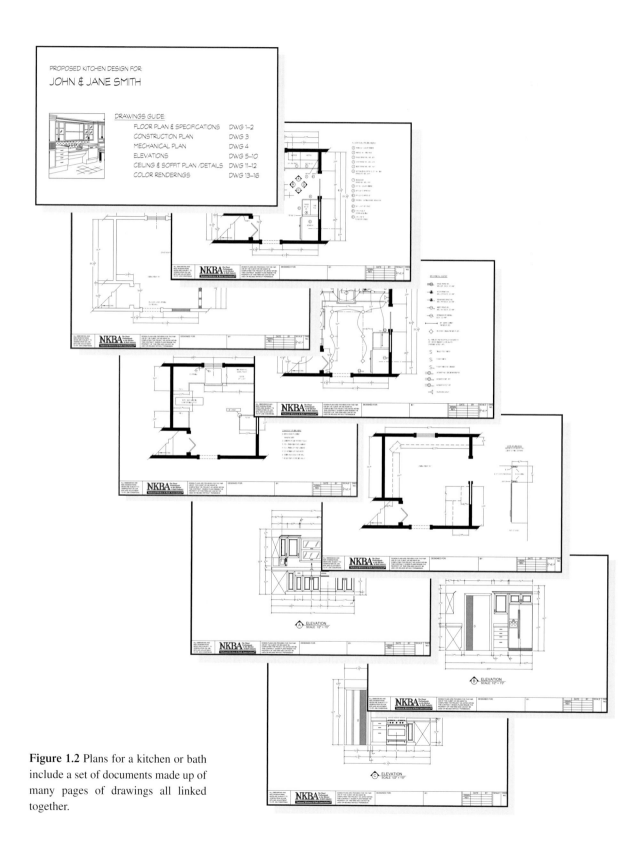

**Figure 1.2** Plans for a kitchen or bath include a set of documents made up of many pages of drawings all linked together.

## Title Page

A cover page to a set of project documents is called a title page and may include any or all of the following: client or building name, location, designer's name and design firm's name, a key to the symbols for materials, and an index of the drawings. It may also include an illustration.

PROPOSED KITCHEN DESIGN FOR:

# JOHN & JANE SMITH

DRAWINGS GUIDE:

| | |
|---|---|
| FLOOR PLAN & SPECIFICATIONS | DWG 1–2 |
| CONSTRUCTION PLAN | DWG 3 |
| MECHANICAL PLAN | DWG 4 |
| ELEVATIONS | DWG 5–10 |
| CEILING & SOFFIT PLAN /DETAILS | DWG 11–12 |
| COLOR RENDERINGS | DWG 13–16 |

## Kitchen and Bath Plans

The floor plan is the central reference point for all the other drawings in the set of documents. A floor plan is an overhead cut-away view of the room. It generally depicts the entire room and shows all major structural elements such as walls, door swings, door openings, partitions, windows and archways. It also shows cabinet, appliance and fixture placement, dimensions, nomenclature and other necessary notes.

**Figure 1.3** A cover page to a set of project documents is called the title page. It includes the client's name, a list of drawings and perhaps an interpretive sketch of the project.

The floor plan, and other kitchen and bath drawings, is drawn at a scale of $^1/_2" = 1'\text{-}0"$ to provide the required level of detail. The dimensions written on the plans are exact and are always used when reading a plan. Do not use a ruler to determine dimensions from a plan. This is because the size of the plan itself can change slightly during duplication. Or, the drawings may not be perfectly to scale, in which case there may be a notation "NTS" (Not to Scale) in the title block.

On the plan, various types of lines (different thicknesses, broken or solid etc,) plus various symbols and words are all used to convey information about the room. (These are all explained in Chapter 3.) Letters within circular arrows on the floor plan link to another type of drawing of each wall called an elevation.

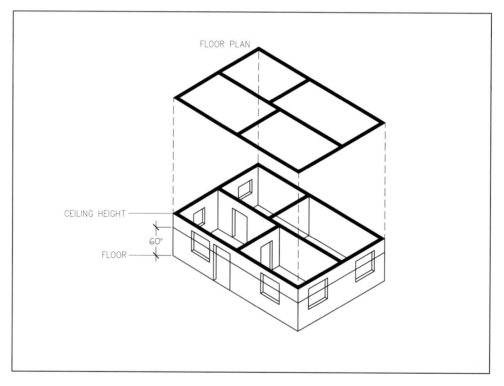

**Figure 1.4** Floor plan "lifted" from top or ceiling.

The floor plan is used as a visual index to locate the specifics of each area of the room. The circled numbers on the floor plan correspond to a numbered list of product details. These lists are called a schedule or specifications and they spell out details such as cabinet sizes, appliances, fixtures, etc.

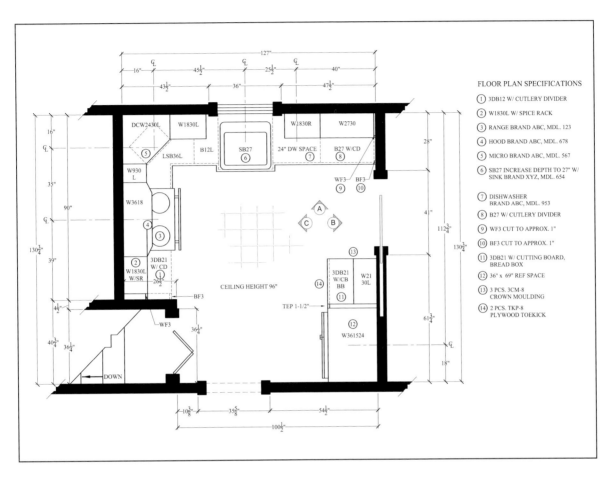

FLOOR PLAN SPECIFICATIONS

1. 3DB12 W/ CUTLERY DIVIDER
2. W1830L W/ SPICE RACK
3. RANGE BRAND ABC, MDL. 123
4. HOOD BRAND ABC, MDL. 678
5. MICRO BRAND ABC, MDL. 567
6. SB27 INCREASE DEPTH TO 27" W/ SINK BRAND XYZ, MDL. 654
7. DISHWASHER BRAND ABC, MDL. 953
8. B27 W/ CUTLERY DIVIDER
9. WF3 CUT TO APPROX. 1"
10. BF3 CUT TO APPROX. 1"
11. 3DB21 W/ CUTTING BOARD, BREAD BOX
12. 36" x 69" REF SPACE
13. 3 PCS. 3CM-8 CROWN MOULDING
14. 2 PCS. TKP-8 PLYWOOD TOEKICK

If walls or openings need to be altered from their original locations, a drawing called a construction plan is required. It shows both the existing conditions of the structure and the changes to be made to achieve the design. Special symbols, as seen in Chapter 3, are used to clearly illustrate construction alterations.

**Figure 1.5** An example of a typical kitchen floor plan showing cabinet and appliance placement, dimensions, nomenclature and other necessary notes. (Concept by Mary Galloway, CKD–Alexandria, Virginia)

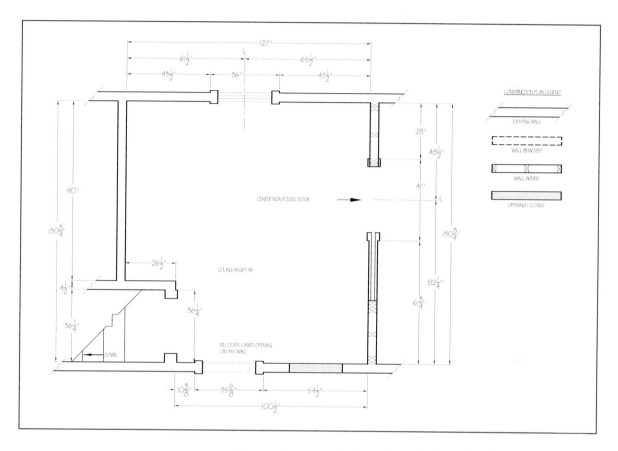

**Figure 1.6** An example of a typical construction plan showing new walls and one existing wall to be removed. (Concept by Mary Galloway, CKD–Alexandria, Virginia)

The construction plan includes only the walls, their dimensions and a legend explaining what the symbols represent.

The mechanical plan is one or more drawings showing the arrangement of the heating, ventilation, air conditioning, plumbing, lighting and electrical systems. Because many of these trades are themselves specialized, mechanical plans may at first seem difficult to understand. As shown in Chapter 3, there are different symbols to indicate lights, switches, plumbing, heating, air conditioning and ventilation systems. A legend included on a mechanical plan describes what each symbol means. The details of the mechanical systems are kept separate from the details of the floor plan. However, the locations of the cabinets, countertops and fixtures are noted for placement only.

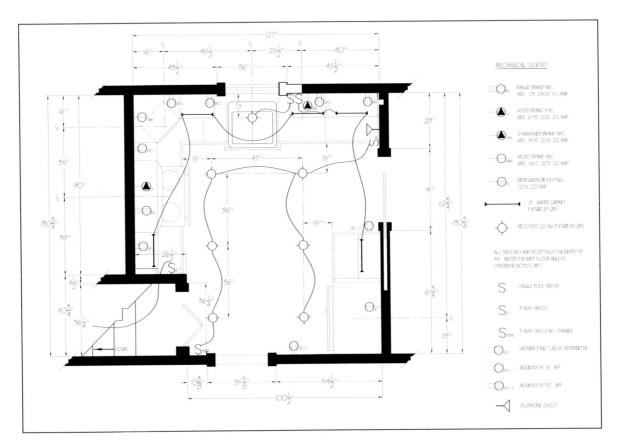

Figure 1.7 A typical mechanical plan showing plumbing, lighting and electrical, heating and ventilation information. Note the legend describing the symbols. (Concept by Mary Galloway, CKD–Alexandria, Virginia)

It is important for you to understand mechanical plans, because as you create a design, you may need to ask a question like, "Is there any flexibility in the plumbing supply line, drain or vent locations?" Most likely you will not illustrate the entire heating and air conditioning system, but you do need to identify where the vents are, and should be aware of where the ducting is within the structure and how it will affect your design.

## Interpretive Drawings

An interpretive drawing is one that helps visualize what the finished project will look like. Interpretive drawings are used as an explanatory means of understanding the floor plan, but never substitute for floor plans. The most common interpretive drawings are elevations and perspectives.

The elevation drawing is a vertical projection of one exterior side of a building or one wall of a room. It is drawn to scale in height and in width, but not in depth.

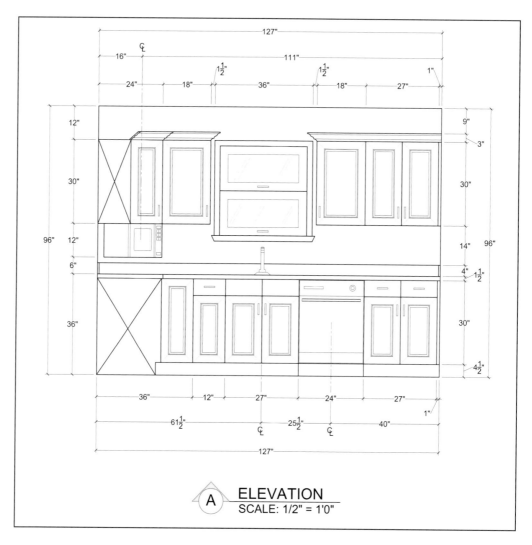

ELEVATION
SCALE: 1/2" = 1'0"

**Figure 1.8** A typical elevation drawing showing one wall of a kitchen with the dimensions on all four sides. It is to scale in height and width, but does not convey any depth. (Concept by Mary Galloway, CKD–Alexandria, Virginia)

Several elevations are generally needed to properly illustrate the room. Each elevation has a symbol (usually a letter such as "A," "B," "C") which corresponds to the same letter on the floor plan indicating the wall depicted in the elevation.

An elevation illustrates a front view of all wall areas where cabinets and equipment will be, as detailed on the floor plan. Cabinets, countertops, fixtures and equipment in the elevation are all dimensioned.

The perspective drawing provides a three-dimensional view of the space. The realistic appearance of a perspective makes it the ideal type of interpretive drawing because it most closely resembles what the human eye sees. The perspective relies on the appearance of the space, giving depth to the items in the space, and is not drawn to scale.

Think of a perspective as if you are standing in the middle of railroad tracks. The sides of the tracks seem to meet and touch each other in the distance, but you know they do not. This point at which they seem to touch is called a vanishing point. The various types of perspective drawings are explained in Chapter 4.

**Figure 1.9** A perspective drawing provides a three-dimensional view of the room. The drawing closely resembles how the human eye sees a space. (Courtesy of NKBA)

### Section Drawings

A section drawing is a "slice" of a building, showing the inner construction of walls, furniture or any element that needs clarification. In a kitchen or bathroom, this type of drawing may also be done to show a cut-away view of cabinetry, molding, soffits or backsplashes. Some details may be small, but reveal important relationships of materials which cannot be communicated on a floor plan or elevation. For instance, a countertop with a custom edge might need to be detailed because of the way it will be fastened to the cabinets.

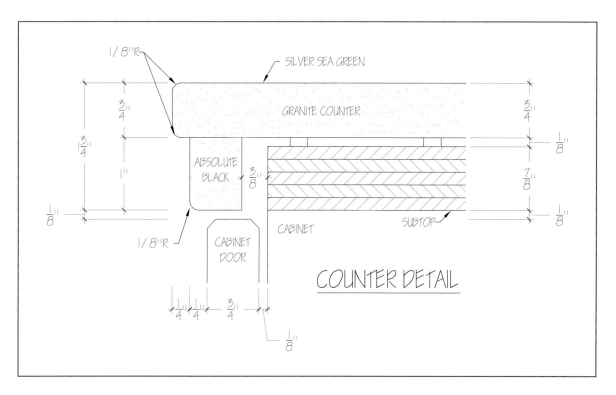

**Figure 1.10** A section drawing showing a cut-away view of a counter-top and how it relates to the cabinet. (Courtesy of Leslie Cohen, CKD–Encinitas, California)

Section drawings can be set on the same page as the floor plan or may be collected on pages of their own. A detail shows a specific part of the project drawn at $3/4$-inch or 1-inch scale because it may have too much information to show on a smaller scale.

A separate countertop plan is helpful to illustrate the installation or fabrication to the allied tradesperson, particularly in complex projects, such as those that combine various counter materials or built-up edge treatments. A countertop plan shows only the walls of the space, the outline of the cabinets, fixtures and equipment, applicable notes, details and dimensions. A detailed profile of the counter edge treatment is often provided at a larger scale to clearly illustrate the counter design and its overhang relative to the face of the cabinet or an indication of inset doors.

A drawing showing the space above the wall cabinets is called a soffit plan and is required when the soffit is a different depth than the wall or tall cabinet below it. It is also recommended when the soffit is to be installed prior to the wall or tall cabinets.

If the soffit is a complex design, cabinets may not need to be shown. An elevation of the soffit is included on the soffit plan to further detail complex designs.

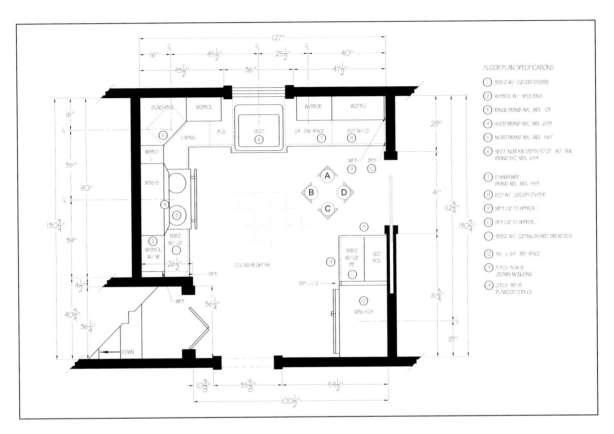

FLOOR PLAN SPECIFICATIONS

1. SDB2 W/ CUTLERY DIVIDER
2. W.85OL W/ SPICE RACK
3. RANGE BRAND ABC, MDL 123
4. HOOD BRAND ABC, MDL 678
5. MICRO BRAND ABC, MDL 567
6. SB27 INCREASE DEPTH TO 27 W/ SINK BRAND XYZ, MDL 654
7. DISHWASHER BRAND ABC, MDL 963
8. B27 W/ CUTLERY DIVIDER
9. WF3 CUT TO APPROX 1
10. BF3 CUT TO APPROX
11. SDB2 W/ CUTTING BOARD, BREAD BOX
12. 36 x 69 REF SPACE
13. 3 PCS 3CM-8 CROWN MOLDING
14. 2 PCS 1KP-8 PLYWOOD TOEKICK

## Schedule and Specifications

A schedule is a group of pages within the plans which have lists of like items specified for the home, such as cabinets, appliances, etc. A reference number circled on the plan corresponds to a number on the schedule. It can be considered a short form of specifications and is a quick way to find information at the job site.

Written documents accompanying the plans are called the specifications or "specs." These are descriptions, in words, of the materials and products to be used and the quality expected. For example, appliances and plumbing fixtures are specified by brand and model number. Or, the grade of wood that is to be installed in the flooring is spelled out.

The specifications can be either on the plans or a separate document if they will complicate the drawing. Because specifications give more detailed expectations of quality and quantity of materials than would be possible in illustrated plans, they need to be carefully reviewed when the kitchen or bath designer is copying the information needed from these specifications. This process is called a take-off.

**Figure 1.11** Specifications are included on the right hand side of this floor plan and call out appliance brands and models, as well as other product details. (Concept by Mary Galloway, CKD–Alexandria, Virginia)

### Design Statement

One project document not used as frequently as in the past is a design statement. A design statement is the designer's opportunity to explain what was changed in the space, why it was changed and how it was changed. In 250 to 500 words, a one page description of the project helps pull together the thought process and reasoning of the designer's solution to the client's challenge.

A design statement should be concise and clearly outline the challenges the designer faced and overcame such as budget, construction constraints, client requests and lifestyle. Aesthetic choices should also be included to complete the presentation of the project. The key to a successful design statement is to keep it brief and interesting. Examples of design statements are found in Chapter 8.

With all of these documents for one project, it may seem as though not every person involved in the job needs to see each one in the set. But this is not the case. Regardless of an individual's focus, each person needs to be responsible for reviewing the entire set of documents. For example, if the electrician is not given a set of cabinet drawings, but only sees the electrical plans, he will not know about a decorative backsplash that will interfere with outlet placement. And although clients may be most interested in a perspective, it is their responsibility to sign off on all technical drawings as well.

### Other Drawings for Review Only

In addition to the set of kitchen and bath documents you create, there are related project documents, drawn by others, that you may need to read and review. These can include a full set of house plans or architectural drawings, site plans and structural plans.

Although everyone in the building industry communicates via plans, different professionals use different versions of this common language. Drawings done by architects and interior designers, while using many of the same symbols as kitchen and bath drawings, are not the same.

Generally an architectural floor plan shows the entire building or project.

You may need to refer to architectural drawings for information that could affect your kitchen or bath design. For example, it is helpful to have separate floor plans for each level of the house, in addition to the level where the kitchen or bathroom is located, because your new scheme for a kitchen or bath may affect the spaces above and below it. There are times when an idea will not be possible because of the impact it may have on the other levels.

There are several major differences between architectural plans and kitchen and bathroom plans.

First, is the difference in scale. Architectural drawings are done on a smaller scale of $1/4$" to one foot (1' 0") in order to show the whole building, rather than the larger scale of $1/2$" to one foot (1' 0") used in kitchen and bath drawings. (Be sure the client understands that a drawing done at $1/2$" scale will give the illusion of a bigger space.)

Another difference is the height indicated in the drawings. Most architectural plans are drawn as if the space is cut at a height between 48 and 60 inches above the floor. However, if kitchen and bath plans were drawn based on this height, many cabinets and other important details above these heights would be left out. Therefore, kitchen and bathroom plans are drawn from the actual ceiling height so that all cabinets, counters, appliances, fixtures and other details are shown.

As you learn more about measuring rooms and dimensioning plans later in this book, you will see that it is the standard of the kitchen and bath industry to measure or dimension finished walls only. This standard has been established because of the critical fit of the products specified for the space.

Architectural plans indicate dimensions from the center of partitions and support columns. Architects follow this dimensioning process because building materials, such as lumber, may vary in thickness, and so the center point will always remain standard.

On kitchen and bathroom plans, however, sinks and all major appliances are positioned by the center of the item to determine its rough-in placement. Interior designers have their own drawing standards, especially with regards to centering, which usually focuses on centering windows.

Another type of plan you may need to review is a site plan or plot plan which is an overhead view of the property around the building. You may want to verify that a new kitchen or bath addition will not come too close to property lines. Or you may want to know how the orientation of the building affects the kitchen or bathroom.

A drawing which shows how the building is affixed to the concrete walls below is called a footings and foundations drawing. In a remodeling project, you will need to find out if the walls surrounding the kitchen are load bearing walls or non-structural partitions. You may need a structural framing plan to illustrate just that. If your design calls for removing a wall, you need to understand how to make certain the structure remains secure and how it will remain secure.

# Chapter 2: Measuring the Design Space: The Steps to Accurate Measurements

Before drafting the project documents, carefully inspect and measure the space to be designed. Measurements must be accurate to ensure the products selected will fit. Inspect the space and any surrounding area that will be affected by the installation.

Before leaving to measure the job site, whether it is new construction or a remodel, think about the following:

- Have you confirmed the date and time to measure the job?

- Is the job site ready to be measured?

- Do you have a map and/or directions?

- Will you be measuring during the day or at night? An evening appointment to measure will not give you as good an idea of the exterior walls that will be affected.

- Will the client, builder, contractor or anyone else be at the job site during your visit?

- Do you need assistance from someone in your company?

- Do you have a cellular phone or other means of communication should you need assistance from someone not on the job site?

Do you have a client survey or a list of questions to ask the clients? (Complete client surveys can be found in *Kitchen Planning* and *Bath Planning*. Both books are part of NKBA's *Professional Resource Library*.) You'll need to find out how they live, what they like, what kind of storage they need and much more. These are additional reminders for a remodeling job:

- Call one or two days prior to confirm the date and time, including how long the measuring process will take.

- Arrive no earlier than five minutes before the scheduled time because the client may not be ready.

- Park your vehicle where it will not block or impede the client's parking space.

- Be considerate of the client's home and remove your shoes or cover them.

- Ask for permission before playing with or picking up small children or animals.

- Refrain from using the client's bathroom.

- Ask client to remove valuable items that might be in the way of measuring. Also be mindful of the client's property and avoid any unnecessary handling of personal objects.

- Ask for permission to open all existing cabinets to look for hidden obstructions, pipes and wires.

- Avoid any distractions and concentrate fully. Politely ask the client to refrain from conversation while you measure the space.

- Carefully and accurately measure and re-measure all walls without client interruption.

- Take photographs of existing walls for future reference during the design process.

- If conditions are questionable, it is acceptable to schedule another appointment to measure the job when you can bring/meet someone to help you, i.e. a plumber or electrician.

- Finish measuring at or before the time you originally told the client you would.

- Schedule the next appointment and discuss what the next step should be.

Also for measuring a new construction job site, consider the following:

- Take into account the job site conditions, the weather conditions and the task of measuring a new structure. You may need to wear a hard hat, boots and have a four wheel drive vehicle. A woman should refrain from wearing a skirt as it may impede the ability to measure properly. Also many times, new construction jobs have areas that make it difficult or impossible to measure while wearing a skirt, for instance, climbing makeshift stairs in the form of a ladder or crossing a trench around the perimeter of the structure.

- How safe is the job site environment?

- Are the floor plans and job folder available?

- Are the mechanical systems noted on the floor plans?

Make sure you have the following items. Even if you leave most of them in your car, they will be a lot closer than at your office if you need them.

- Client survey form to be filled in at client's house

- Twenty-five foot metal tape measure with a 1-inch blade

- Six or eight foot folding rule

- Framing square

- Level

- Pencils, pens of different colors or crayons and grease pencils to mark on the floor the layout of the cabinets including nomenclature

- Calculator

- Masking tape

- Angled measuring tool to automatically calculate an angled wall

- Note pad or clipboard with graph paper

- Flashlight

- Digital or video camera

- Hard hat and boots

- Small broom

- Small step ladder

- Business cards

- First aid kit

- Four wheel drive vehicle and hard hat for new construction jobs

| IF YOU CHOOSE TO MEASURE… | YOU MAY HAVE THE ADVANTAGE BECAUSE… | BUT YOU MAY ALSO EXPERIENCE DISADVANTAGES. | KEEP IN MIND THAT … | DEGREE OF ACCURACY |
|---|---|---|---|---|
| Using the floor plans the client created… | The designer can make major changes to the plan to better meet client's needs | The builder and client may make other changes after you order the cabinets and equipment. | All parties must agree to your suggestions before orders are processed. "Rough quote" only at this time. | LOW |
| After stud walls are in place… | The designer can suggest major mechanical changes before the trades start their work. | Openings can still be relocated, but watch for concrete slabs that will affect the plan. Product can be ordered but be careful at this stage. | You must check size of wall coverings, floor materials, trim sizes, etc. Mark location of floor joists, studs, etc. | MEDIUM |
| After drywall is installed… | The utilities are set and most clients will not want to make costly changes at this point. | The client may request changes but not pay for them. Be sure to use change order forms. | You must check for additional wall coverings, floor material, trim sizes, etc. | HIGH |
| Before the remodeling project begins… | You are responsible for the complete project so you will be aware of all changes. | If you are furnishing product only, watch for changes that you did not anticipate. | You will need to check the status of the project on a regular basis. | HIGH |

It is important to measure only in inches, not feet and inches. This is because you will be drawing your plans in inches and noting all dimensions on plans in inches (not feet and inches). For example, a wall is noted as being 127 inches long, not 10 feet and 7 inches. By measuring (and thinking) in inches, you will avoid mistakes that can occur when attempting to convert feet to inches.

## MEASURING THE REMODELING JOB

When preparing for a remodeling job, it's wise to follow a few simple steps to ensure concise and accurate planning.

1. Visually inspect the space and draw a proportionally correct room outline: include all windows and doors and indicate north/south orientation and adjacent room or view information.

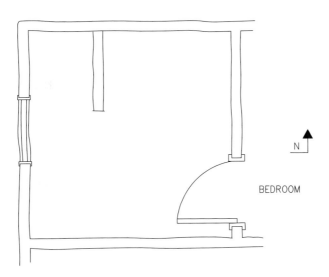

N

BEDROOM

**Figure 2.1** Sketch the space to be designed. (Courtesy of Erica Westeroth, CKD–Toronto, Ontario)

2. Measure the ceiling height in at least three locations. If the heights are not consistent, note the different heights.

- You can mark a midpoint on the wall, measuring from the ceiling down to the mark and then from the mark to the floor.

**Figure 2.2** Mark a midpoint on the wall.

- Or measure from the ceiling down, pushing the tape down with your knee while holding it flat against the wall.

**Figure 2.3** Measure from the ceiling down.

Also a folding rule can be used in the middle of the room where there probably are no obstacles. A folding rule will stay vertical on its own, freeing up your other hand.

- Still another way is to push the tape up from the floor to the ceiling. Repeat at several locations to determine levelness. Record the height in a circle at the center of the floor plan.

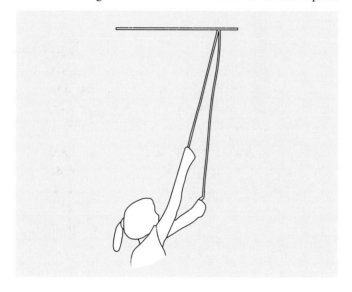

**Figure 2.4** Measure from the floor up.

3. Select a corner as a starting point. If possible, clear a path approximately 36 inches above the floor and measure the full length of the wall. Record the total dimension on the plan. The corner squareness is determined by marking a point 36 inches out from the corner on one wall and 48 inches out from the corner on the adjacent wall and measuring the distance between the two points. If the distance is 60 inches, the corner is square. This formula is known as The Pythagorean Theorem: $A^2 + B^2 = C^2$. Any other measurement indicates the corner is out of square and a note should be made on the plan. A framing square could also be used to determine the squareness of a room.

4. Return to the starting point and measure from the corner to the nearest opening or obstacle (door, window, pipe chase, etc.) and record results. Measure from outside edge to outside edge (of door and window trim) and record the dimension. Continue the process until the opposite corner is reached.

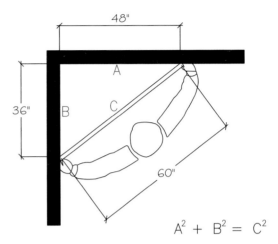

**Figure 2.5** How the Pythagorean Theorem works.

5. Stop and confirm the accuracy of your measurements by comparing the sum of all individual dimensions to the total wall measurement.

6. Repeat steps 3, 4 and 5 for each wall.

7. Complete your client survey form, noting any important dimensions such as window heights from floor and ceiling, door heights, heating, ventilation and air conditioning units.

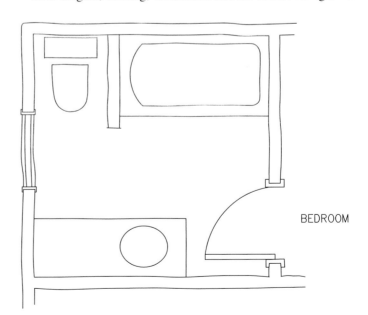

**Figure 2.6** Your sketch now includes doors, windows and other obstacles. (Courtesy of Erica Westeroth, CKD–Toronto, Ontario)

8. Identify plumbing and electrical/lighting centerlines by
returning to the starting point and measuring from corner
to center of outlets, switches, fixtures, appliances, lighting,
venting and plumbing locations. On your sketch, record center
location with standard symbols found in NKBA's Graphics
and Presentations Standards within this book in chapter 7,
as well as the symbols in chapter 3.

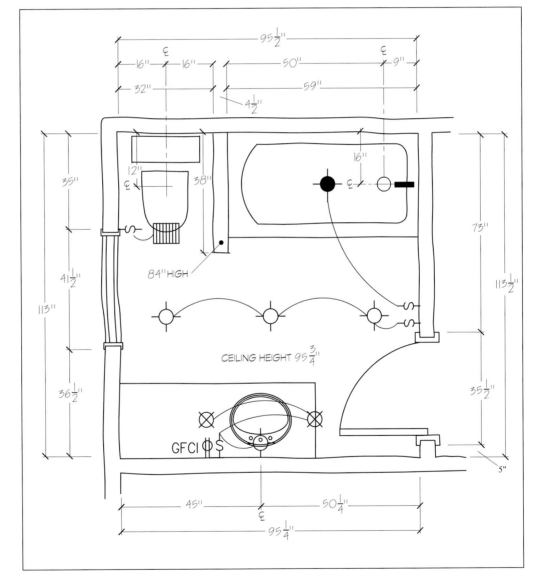

**Figure 2.7** Indicate plumbing and
electrical/lighting on your sketch.
(Courtesy of Erica Westeroth, CKD–
Toronto, Ontario)

9. Make your final inspection. Measure any freestanding furniture pieces, check electrical service panel conditions and check any areas such as basement or attic that may be affected during remodeling.

10. Take photos or videos of the existing space for reference during the design process. Even if you anticipate moving walls or closets, photograph what the space looks like prior to demolition. The photos can also be added to your company's portfolio to show "Before" and "After" images.

## MEASURING NEW CONSTRUCTION

When measuring a new construction site during the framing stages, the process is the same. However, all dimensions will be made from stud wall to stud wall during the job site visit. Architectural elements, such as doors and windows, will be located from stud wall to rough opening. Compare the measurements to the architect's blueprints. If there are discrepancies, discuss them, as well as any consequences to the plan because of changes, with the builder or homeowner.

Verify where doors and windows lead, their size, direction of opening and trim size. Note on the client survey the type and thickness of the material for finishing the walls, ceilings and floors.

After the job site has been measured, adjust the rough dimensions, subtracting finish material and finish depths for each wall surface so that the plan reflects finished wall dimensions. Be sure to confirm what finished materials are to be used before placing any product orders. These finished dimensions can make a big difference in product specifications. Substituting $1/16$-inch thick vinyl with a $3/8$-inch thick marble floor alters the finished floor to ceiling dimension, which in turn affects the heights of tall cabinets and soffits.

# ANGLES AND CURVES

## Angles

Even though an electronic tape measure will automatically measure angled walls, as a designer, you should know how to do it. The most accurate approach is to first lay out a right triangle on the floor in the corner. Measure at least two of its sides and apply the appropriate trigonometric formula. Determine the angle to be found. Then identify the opposite, adjacent and hypotenuse sides of the triangle. The opposite side is the one directly opposite the angle. The hypotenuse is the longest side of the triangle and the remaining leg is termed the adjacent side. Use one of the following trigonometric formulas to determine the angle.

- Sine (SIN) equals the opposite side divided by the hypotenuse.

- Cosine (COS) equals the adjacent side divided by the hypotenuse.

- Tangent (TAN) equals the opposite side divided by the adjacent side.

In our example, the opposite side and hypotenuse are known; therefore the Sine formula is used. Your answer is a decimal number, which should be rounded to the nearest ten thousandth. Then use the Table of Trigonometric Functions (page 26) to find the correct angle. To use the table, look under the appropriate column (SIN, COS or TAN) and find the closest decimal number. Then find the corresponding angle, which is shown at the far left of that row.

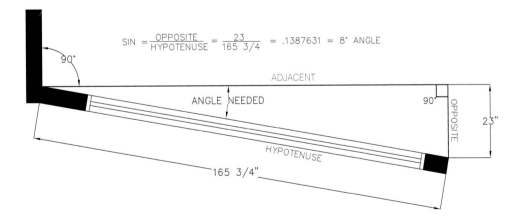

Figure 2.8 Finding an angle.

## Table of Trigonometric Functions

| Degrees | Radian Measure | Sin | Cos | Tan | Degrees | Radian Measure | Sin | Cos | Tan |
|---|---|---|---|---|---|---|---|---|---|
| 0 | 0.00000 | 0.00000 | 1.00000 | 0.00000 | 46 | 0.80285 | 0.71934 | 0.69466 | 1.03553 |
| 1 | 0.01745 | 0.01745 | 0.99985 | 0.01746 | 47 | 0.82030 | 0.73135 | 0.68200 | 1.07237 |
| 2 | 0.03491 | 0.03490 | 0.99939 | 0.03492 | 48 | 0.83776 | 0.74314 | 0.66913 | 1.11061 |
| 3 | 0.05236 | 0.05234 | 0.99863 | 0.05241 | 49 | 0.85521 | 0.75471 | 0.65606 | 1.15037 |
| 4 | 0.06981 | 0.06976 | 0.99756 | 0.06993 | 50 | 0.87266 | 0.76604 | 0.64279 | 1.19175 |
| 5 | 0.08727 | 0.08716 | 0.99619 | 0.08749 | 51 | 0.89012 | 0.77715 | 0.62932 | 1.23490 |
| 6 | 0.10472 | 0.10453 | 0.99452 | 0.10510 | 52 | 0.90757 | 0.78801 | 0.61566 | 1.27994 |
| 7 | 0.12217 | 0.12187 | 0.99255 | 0.12278 | 53 | 0.92502 | 0.79864 | 0.60182 | 1.32704 |
| 8 | 0.13963 | 0.13917 | 0.99027 | 0.14054 | 54 | 0.94248 | 0.80902 | 0.58779 | 1.37638 |
| 9 | 0.15708 | 0.15643 | 0.98769 | 0.15838 | 55 | 0.95993 | 0.81915 | 0.57358 | 1.42815 |
| 10 | 0.17453 | 0.17365 | 0.98481 | 0.17633 | 56 | 0.97738 | 0.82904 | 0.55919 | 1.48256 |
| 11 | 0.19199 | 0.19081 | 0.98163 | 0.19438 | 57 | 0.99484 | 0.83867 | 0.54464 | 1.53986 |
| 12 | 0.20944 | 0.20791 | 0.97815 | 0.21256 | 58 | 1.01229 | 0.84805 | 0.52992 | 1.60033 |
| 13 | 0.22689 | 0.22495 | 0.97437 | 0.23087 | 59 | 1.02974 | 0.85717 | 0.51504 | 1.66428 |
| 14 | 0.24435 | 0.24192 | 0.97030 | 0.24933 | 60 | 1.04720 | 0.86603 | 0.50000 | 1.73205 |
| 15 | 0.26180 | 0.25882 | 0.96593 | 0.26795 | 61 | 1.06465 | 0.87462 | 0.48481 | 1.80405 |
| 16 | 0.27925 | 0.27564 | 0.96126 | 0.28675 | 62 | 1.08210 | 0.88295 | 0.46947 | 1.88073 |
| 17 | 0.29671 | 0.29237 | 0.95630 | 0.30573 | 63 | 1.09956 | 0.89101 | 0.45399 | 1.96261 |
| 18 | 0.31416 | 0.30902 | 0.95106 | 0.32492 | 64 | 1.11701 | 0.89879 | 0.43837 | 2.05030 |
| 19 | 0.33161 | 0.32557 | 0.94552 | 0.34433 | 65 | 1.13446 | 0.90631 | 0.42262 | 2.14451 |
| 20 | 0.34907 | 0.34202 | 0.93969 | 0.36397 | 66 | 1.15192 | 0.91355 | 0.40674 | 2.24604 |
| 21 | 0.36652 | 0.35837 | 0.93358 | 0.38386 | 67 | 1.16937 | 0.92050 | 0.39073 | 2.35585 |
| 22 | 0.38397 | 0.37461 | 0.92718 | 0.40403 | 68 | 1.18682 | 0.92718 | 0.37461 | 2.47509 |
| 23 | 0.40143 | 0.39073 | 0.92050 | 0.42447 | 69 | 1.20428 | 0.93358 | 0.35837 | 2.60509 |
| 24 | 0.41888 | 0.40674 | 0.91355 | 0.44523 | 70 | 1.22173 | 0.93969 | 0.34202 | 2.74748 |
| 25 | 0.43633 | 0.42262 | 0.90631 | 0.46631 | 71 | 1.23918 | 0.94552 | 0.32557 | 2.90421 |
| 26 | 0.45379 | 0.43837 | 0.89879 | 0.48773 | 72 | 1.25664 | 0.95106 | 0.30902 | 3.07768 |
| 27 | 0.47124 | 0.45399 | 0.89101 | 0.50953 | 73 | 1.27409 | 0.95630 | 0.29237 | 3.27085 |
| 28 | 0.48869 | 0.46947 | 0.88295 | 0.53171 | 74 | 1.29154 | 0.96126 | 0.27564 | 3.48741 |
| 29 | 0.50615 | 0.48481 | 0.87462 | 0.55431 | 75 | 1.30900 | 0.96593 | 0.25882 | 3.73205 |
| 30 | 0.52360 | 0.50000 | 0.86603 | 0.57735 | 76 | 1.32645 | 0.97030 | 0.24192 | 4.01078 |
| 31 | 0.54105 | 0.51504 | 0.85717 | 0.60086 | 77 | 1.34390 | 0.97437 | 0.22495 | 4.33148 |
| 32 | 0.55851 | 0.52992 | 0.84805 | 0.62487 | 78 | 1.36136 | 0.97815 | 0.20791 | 4.70463 |
| 33 | 0.57596 | 0.54464 | 0.83867 | 0.64941 | 79 | 1.37881 | 0.98163 | 0.19081 | 5.14455 |
| 34 | 0.59341 | 0.55919 | 0.82904 | 0.67451 | 80 | 1.39626 | 0.98481 | 0.17365 | 5.67128 |
| 35 | 0.61087 | 0.57358 | 0.81915 | 0.70021 | 81 | 1.41372 | 0.98769 | 0.15643 | 6.31375 |
| 36 | 0.62832 | 0.58779 | 0.80902 | 0.72654 | 82 | 1.43117 | 0.99027 | 0.13917 | 7.11537 |
| 37 | 0.64577 | 0.60182 | 0.79864 | 0.75355 | 83 | 1.44862 | 0.99255 | 0.12187 | 8.14435 |
| 38 | 0.66323 | 0.61566 | 0.78801 | 0.78129 | 84 | 1.46608 | 0.99452 | 0.10453 | 9.51436 |
| 39 | 0.68068 | 0.62932 | 0.77715 | 0.80978 | 85 | 1.48353 | 0.99619 | 0.08716 | 11.43005 |
| 40 | 0.69813 | 0.64279 | 0.76604 | 0.83910 | 86 | 1.50098 | 0.99756 | 0.06976 | 14.30067 |
| 41 | 0.71558 | 0.65606 | 0.75471 | 0.86929 | 87 | 1.51844 | 0.99863 | 0.05234 | 19.08114 |
| 42 | 0.73304 | 0.66913 | 0.74314 | 0.90040 | 88 | 1.53589 | 0.99939 | 0.03490 | 28.63625 |
| 43 | 0.75049 | 0.68200 | 0.73135 | 0.93252 | 89 | 1.55334 | 0.99985 | 0.01745 | 57.28996 |
| 44 | 0.76794 | 0.69466 | 0.71934 | 0.96569 | 90 | 1.57080 | 1.00000 | 0.00000 | |
| 45 | 0.78540 | 0.70711 | 0.70711 | 1.00000 | | | | | |

## Curves

Measuring a curved wall requires finding the radius of the curve. Using a yardstick as your straight line, first locate a straight line that terminates at any two points along the curve. This line is referred to as a "chord." Find the rise by determining the exact center of the chord and measuring the perpendicular length from this point to the wall. For kitchen and bathroom planning purposes, a 36-inch chord dimension is recommended because a 36-inch cabinet is the widest unit you should place against a curved wall.

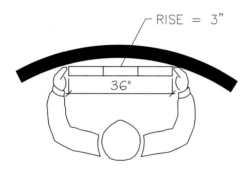

RISE = 3"

36"

**Figure 2.9** Measuring a curved wall.

Use the following formulas to determine the radius:

First find the diameter:

$$((\text{Chord}/2)^2 + \text{Rise}^2)/\text{Rise} = \text{Diameter}$$

Then find the radius:

$$\frac{\text{Diameter}}{2} = \text{Radius}$$

For example, if you were to use a yardstick (36 inches) as a chord and found the rise to be three inches, the formula would be calculated as follows:

$$\frac{(\frac{1}{2}(36))^2 + 3^2}{3} \Rightarrow \frac{18^2 + 3^2}{3} \Rightarrow \frac{324 + 9}{3} \Rightarrow \frac{333}{3} \Rightarrow 111 \text{ is the Diameter}$$

$$\frac{111}{2} \Rightarrow 55\frac{1}{2}" \text{ is the Radius}$$

Now that the radius is established, the length of the curve (referred to as the arc below) can be determined with the following formula:

$$A = \frac{\pi \times r \times <}{180}$$

where A = length of the arc or curve

$\pi$ = "pi" which is 3.14

r = Radius

< = Angle

x = Multiply

## TIPS FROM THE PROS

The kitchen and bathroom designer needs to thoroughly understand a set of drawings before beginning the take-off. Seasoned experts in the kitchen and bath industry share the following hints.

- Never plan a room that will have furniture in it without first knowing the size of the furniture and where it will be placed.

- When you are doing a hardware take-off, be methodical. For example, when you are doing a take-off for cabinet and entry doors, start by counting the number of doors in the entire plan or refer to the door schedule. Make sure you end up with that number of doors and corresponding hardware when you finish your take-off. Consider dividing the doors by groups: cabinets, key lock, passage and privacy. Then count the hardware by areas and total to check quantity. Missing items during the take-off is very costly in terms of reordering, delay time and frustration. Check and double check!

- If you add any items that are not on the schedule, consider whether they will change the plans. For example, if you decide to add a barbeque in an island, you have now changed the mechanical plans. You may need to add electrical and/or gas supply, along with ductwork for ventilation. Any changes in framing, electrical, plumbing or construction that products require must be clearly communicated to the builder or architect so that the appropriate notes can be incorporated into the plans.

# Chapter 3: Get Ready to Draft:
# The Tools & Techniques of Hand Drafting

## THE TOOLS

Just as an installer needs the right tools to build a kitchen or bathroom, a draftsperson needs the right tools to put the design on paper. Purchase the best quality equipment you can afford. The following is a list of drafting tools you will need to draft your design by hand. Your list of tools will grow as your drafting style and needs grow. You should be able to find all of these items at a drafting or art supply store or even an office supply store. Or search for "drafting supplies" on the Internet to find a large selection.

- Drafting paper, also known as vellum
- Drafting tracing paper
- Drafting lead holder and leads in a variety of weights or hardness
- Pencil pointer
- Drafting board, either portable or stationary
- T-square, parallel bar or drafting machine
- Triangles, 30° x 60°, 45° and adjustable
- Architect's scale with $1/4$-inch and $1/2$-inch scales
- Templates that include kitchen appliances and bathroom fixtures are shown in $1/2$-inch scale
- Drafting tape or drafting dots
- Erasers
- Erasing shield
- Dusting brush
- Compass
- Curves
- Plan enhancements (i.e. stick-on ready artwork)
- Inking pens
- Electric eraser
- Lettering guide
- Markers and colored pencils

**Figure 3.1** Typical drafting tools. (Courtesy of Alvin & Co., Inc.)

The one tool that will be discussed in its own chapter is software developed specifically for kitchen and bathroom design and computer-aided design (CAD) software. Technology has made designing and drafting kitchen and bathroom plans faster and easier and so computer-aided drawing requires a thorough review.

## SELECTING AND USING TOOLS

Professional drawing presentations require special drafting paper. The paper most often used is called vellum. This is translucent paper with high strength and is usually reserved for the final drawings that will be presented to the client. Tracing paper, sometimes referred to as "onion skin" or "trash paper," is used in the design concept stage and discarded once the final drawings are completed.

**Figure 3.2** NKBA vellum paper.

**Figure 3.3** There are many pencils and leads to choose from. Which to use depends on personal preference. (Courtesy of Alvin & Co., Inc.)

The selection of pencils and leads is important. Most drafts people avoid wooden-cased drawing pencils, preferring a drafting lead holder. The holder acts as a shell for the lead and enables you to easily push the lead out for convenient sharpening. There are also mechanical pencils that hold very thin leads, which do not require any sharpening. These save time and eliminate the extra tool. However, the line quality is limited to the thickness of the lead and thin leads will break often until you become accustomed to applying just the right amount of pressure.

The seventeen varieties of leads are classified by degrees of hardness and identified by a letter and/or number. Experiment to discover which lead hardness works best for you. The softer leads, such as 2B and 3B, are recommended for pencil renderings with shades and shadows because they are darker. The softer the lead is, the easier it flows and the more it smears.

Harder leads such as 2H produce a crisp line that will not smear as much, but the lines are much lighter and the leads dent the paper, making them difficult to erase. Leads are further classified by thickness: .03 mm, .05mm, .07mm, .09mm and 2mm. Most drafting is done with the 2mm size, but lettering and fine details should be done with a thinner lead like a .05mm.

Keeping a sharp point on the lead is one of the key elements in developing good line-work. To keep a sharp point, rotate the pencil as you draw.

| | |
|---|---|
| 9H | Extremely hard |
| 8H | |
| 7H | |
| 6H | Hard |
| 5H | |
| 4H | |
| 3H | |
| 2H | |
| H | |
| F | Mid-range hardness |
| HB | |
| B | |
| 2B | |
| 3B | |
| 4B | Soft |
| 5B | |
| 6B | Extremely soft |

**Figure 3.4** Drafting lead hardness chart.

**Figure 3.5** Portable drafting boards are available through NKBA and other drafting and drawing supply stores. (Courtesy of Alvin & Co., Inc.)

Your drafting board should accommodate the largest size drawing paper you normally use. The surface of the board should be perfectly smooth and constructed so as not to warp or bend. If you use a T-square, the working edge (left or right-handedness) of the board must be straight and true. A 10° to 15° slope will provide a comfortable drawing surface, as well as a clear view of your work in progress. For used or worn surfaces, or to protect new surfaces, fasten a vinyl covering on the board surface. The common brand names for this material are "Vyco" and "Borco."

**Figure 3.6** Stationary drafting tables come in a variety of styles. (Courtesy of Alvin & Co., Inc.)

**Figure 3.7** The T-square.

The T-square/parallel bar is the most economical form of drafting straightedge equipment. It is used to draw horizontal lines and to keep the drawing square.

Hold a T-square firmly against one edge of the board while sliding it vertically along that edge to position your triangle to draw vertical lines and to draw horizontal lines using the T-square itself. Use only the top edge of the T-square for drawing lines. The bottom edge may not be parallel with the top edge and could result in an out-of-square drawing if both edges are used. To check the T-square for straightness, draw a line from the left edge of the T-square to its right edge. Turn the T-square over and draw another line beginning at the same location. If there is a difference of more than $1/16$ of an inch at any location, the T-square should not be used.

Some kitchen and bathroom designers prefer a parallel bar drafting system. The parallel bar works similarly to the T-square but is permanently attached to the drafting board. The parallel bar attaches to the corners of the board with wires that glide on pulleys. Errors are limited with a parallel bar because it is not handed and therefore is more likely to stay square. Wires kept tight and in good condition will last longer than those that are not.

For the best quality drafting, use a drafting machine or "arm." These are expensive but enable the user to draw horizontal, vertical or any other angled line without additional equipment. There are various models available ranging from the compact, clip-on types to larger V-track types. A drafting machine offers the highest level of linear accuracy possible. Straightedge attachments allow flexibility in working with different scales or changing from the imperial to the metric system.

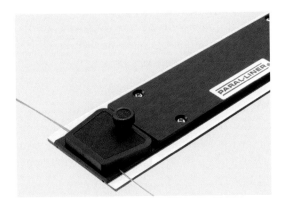

**Figure 3.8** You may prefer a parallel bar drafting system...
(Courtesy of Alvin & Co., Inc.)

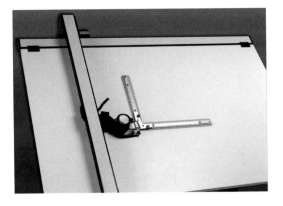

**Figure 3.9** ...or a drafting machine to ensure the most accuracy. (Courtesy of Alvin & Co., Inc.)

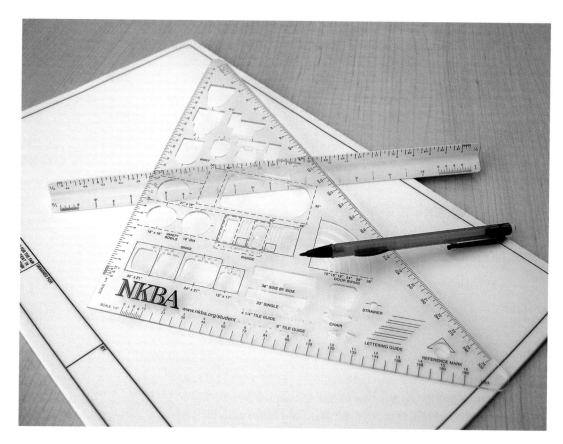

**Figure 3.10** NKBA triangle with kitchen and bathroom template. (Courtesy of NKBA)

A necessary drafting tool is a three-sided plastic piece called a triangle. Some triangles also include kitchen appliances and equipment template outlines. A combination kitchen and bathroom triangle/template is available through NKBA.

Triangles are used with both T-squares and parallel bars to draw vertical and angular lines. The triangle rests on the horizontal straight edge to ensure that vertical lines will be perpendicular to the horizontal lines. The two most common triangles are: 45° and 30° x 60°. The degrees indicate the angles of the triangle.

Look for triangles made of clear or tinted plastic with eased or beveled edges. The tinted plastic is easier to see and reduces shadows caused by overhead lighting. The beveled or eased edge makes the triangle easier to pick up and is absolutely necessary when inking a drawing: the ink will not bleed under the triangle when done correctly.

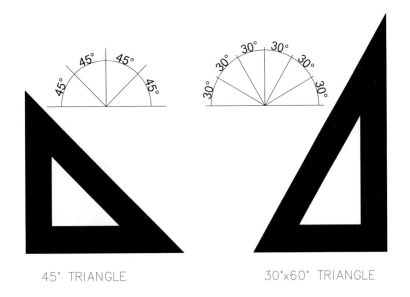

45° TRIANGLE                30°x60° TRIANGLE

**Figure 3.11** 45° and 30°x60° triangles.

Triangles may be used in conjunction with a T-square or parallel bar to draw vertical lines. Begin by holding the T-square firmly and placing the triangle horizontally along the upper edge of the T-square. Slide the triangle into position and hold it with your left or right hand, and pull the pencil upward along the vertical edge.

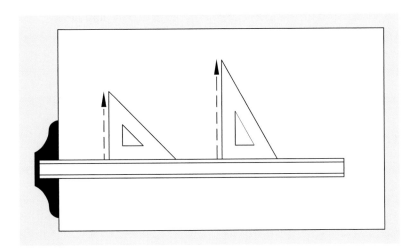

**Figure 3.12** Draw vertical lines from the bottom of the triangle upwards.

35

The same process is used to draw lines at angles. Locate the triangle and pull the pencil from the left to right if right-handed (right to left if left-handed) always gradually rotating the pencil between your fingers. This will ensure the most accurate and consistent line work. The most common angles, 75, 60, 45, 30 and 15 degrees, are easily drawn with the two triangles mentioned. If odd angles are required, an adjustable triangle can be set at the desired angle.

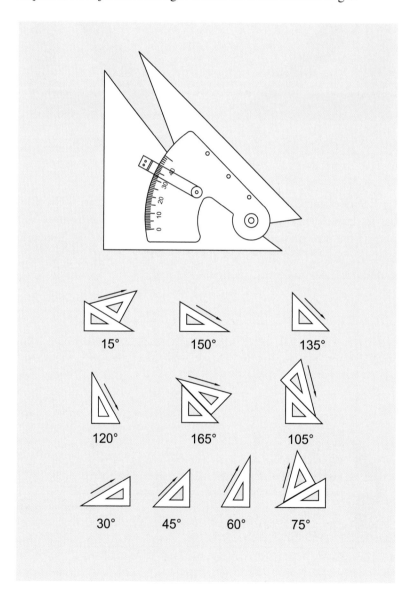

**Figure 3.13** Draw a number of angles by combining triangles or using an adjustable model.

To check the accuracy of a 90° angle of a triangle, draw a vertical line from its bottom to its top point. Turn the triangle over and draw another line beginning at the same location as the first line. If there is a difference of more than $1/32$ inch at the top of an eight-inch line, the triangle should not be used.

An architect's scale is used to measure and scale a drawing. The most common type is a triangular shaped bar that offers eleven different scales in feet and inches. For your kitchen and bathroom plans, all drawings will be done at the scale of $1/2" = 1'-0"$ or 1 cm = 20 cm. Flat models with four scales are also available. These are sometimes preferred because they eliminate time spent hunting for the right scale on a triangular shaped type.

**Figure 3.14** An architect's scale. (Courtesy of Alvin & Co., Inc.)

To accurately measure with a scale, first select the proper scale size and place it on the drawing parallel with the line to be measured. Be careful to note which direction to measure: some scales show the number of full feet to the right of zero and then show inches to the left of zero. However there are some scales, such as on the NKBA template, where you start at zero and count inches and feet in the same direction.

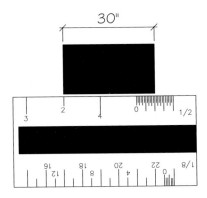

**Figure 3.15** Measuring 30" using a $1/2$" scale where the inches are on the right side of zero and feet are on the left.

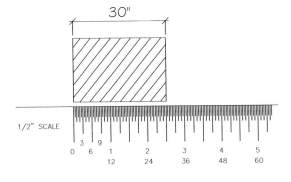

**Figure 3.16** Measuring 30" using a $1/2$" scale where feet and inches are to the right of zero.

37

Templates for plan and elevation views are available for almost everything: kitchen appliances and equipment, bathroom fixtures, door swings, circles and ellipses. Many templates are available in drafting supply stores and are designed for architects in $1/8$ inch to $1/4$ inch scales. As a kitchen and bathroom specialist, you will need $1/2$ inch scaled templates that may be available from the cabinet, appliance and plumbing manufacturers you supply or specify. Using templates saves time and produces a consistent, professional-looking drawing.

Drafting tape holds your drawing in place while you work. Drafting tape is easily removed, unlike masking or Scotch tape which will tear the paper. Drafting tape can be purchased in a variety of widths and in packages with easy tear-off cutting edges. Also available are drafting "dots;" these are round pieces of tape, similar to stickers, which peel off a roll. The dots are convenient to use and are less likely to roll up after the T-square or parallel bar has passed over them a few times if pressed firmly with the edge with your finger nail to ensure they adhere to the paper.

Changing your mind and your design is a major part of the planning process. This makes choosing the appropriate eraser and using the proper technique as important as drawing a line correctly. The wrong eraser may stain or even tear the paper.

Look for a soft eraser, such as the Pink-Pearl or White Vinyl-lite brands available in convenient holders that can be refilled much like a lead holder. When erasing, be sure to hold the paper tightly in place and apply only as much pressure as necessary. For hard-to-remove lines, place a smooth, hard surface under the area to be erased (a plastic triangle works well). Some leads will seem to bleed through vellum paper or at least dent the paper if too much pressure is applied.

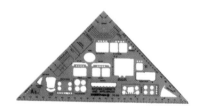

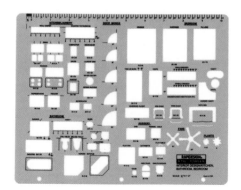

**Figure 3.17** Examples of templates. (Courtesy of Alvin & Co., Inc.)

Turning the paper over and erasing the area on the back will sometimes remove the marks and dents. If you choose to ink your drawings, an electric eraser will become one of your most used tools, saving you time and improving the quality of your presentations. Electric erasers are lightweight and cordless. However, excessive erasing can wear a hole through the paper, so use this tool carefully.

**Figure 3.18** Using an erasing shield allows you to erase only what you want.

An erasing shield is a small, thin piece of metal with various shaped holes, used to isolate a specific area of the drawing to be erased, eliminating over erasing and redrawing. A dusting brush typically has a handle with long, soft bristles made of nylon or horsehair and is used for removing eraser shavings and graphite particles from the drawing without smudging. A brush is necessary to keep your drawing clean and clear of debris.

Use a compass to draw circles or arcs that are not on your templates. Most compasses will produce circles with diameters ranging from $3/16$ inch to 13 inches. One end of this tool has an adjustable needle point and the other a lead point. To keep the circle radius consistent, the pencil lead end must be sharpened in a beveled fashion with the beveled edge facing out. To sharpen the pencil lead point, rub the bevel side back and forth along sandpaper. The bevel point should be between $1/64$ inch to $1/32$ inch shorter than the needle point. While drawing the curve, hold the compass perpendicular to the paper with a light touch to avoid making a hole in the paper. Special attachments are also available for replacing the lead with an ink pen-point.

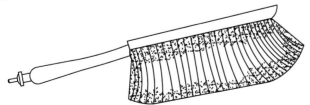

**Figure 3.19** Use a dusting brush to remove eraser shavings and graphite from your pencil rather than your hand which may smear the drawing.

**Figure 3.20** Irregular or French curves.

Irregular curves, commonly referred to as "French" curves, are used to draw curved lines other than circles or arcs. A clear or tinted piece of plastic with several curves, including small, large and a few long slightly curved edges, is recommended. To draw an irregular curve, plot several points through which the curve must pass, and then select the curved edge which most closely matches.

For complex curved lines, more points will be necessary and the curve may have to be drawn in sections, rotating and moving the irregular curve until the desired curvilinear line is completed. Flexible curves are also available. These are wires covered in a rubber-like material which can be positioned to fit almost any large, curved shape.

Plan enhancements are sheets of press-on or stick-on lettering, symbols, people, accessories and shading that make it easy to graphically enhance drawings. Lettering machines also enhance the plan by enabling you to type out letters or numbers onto clear sticky-back tape which you apply directly to the drawing. The press-on lettering takes more time and precision to mount. The edges of the tape are noticeable on original drawings; however, if blueprints or

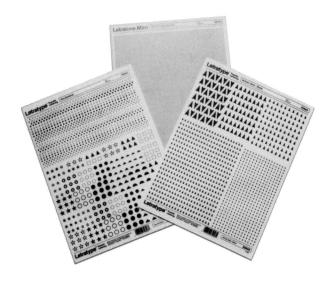

**Figure 3.21** Use press-on or stick-on lettering, symbols and shading to enhance drawings.

photocopies are going to be used, the edges can be almost invisible if the machine is set on a lighter setting. Symbols such as electrical arrows, plants, trees and dot shading are also available in sticky-back or press-on sheets.

An inking pen is one of the easiest and most economical ways to improve the quality of your drawings. In the past, inking a drawing was time-consuming and required skill because the only tool available was a ruling pen, which works like a fountain pen. They were hard to control because the ink was easily smeared and could unexpectedly drip onto the drawing. The technical pens available today eliminate these worries. Although it still takes a bit of practice and the ink will smear if rubbed too soon, inking can be learned. The technical pen is engineered to allow ink to flow out only when it is needed. Some pens are available with snap-on ink cartridge refills, virtually eliminating any handling of messy ink.

The first rule of inking is to use a straightedge with a slightly raised or beveled edge to eliminate ink bleeding under your tools. You will find proper maintenance of your pen vital, which means it should be emptied and cleaned after each use. Cleaning solutions and ultrasonic machines similar to those used for cleaning jewelry are specially formulated to remove clogged ink.

A lettering guide is used to draw guide lines for lettering. By placing the pencil lead in the appropriate hole, the draftsperson can quickly layout consistently even guide lines without measuring. The floor plan specification list is a good place to use a lettering guide.

A.

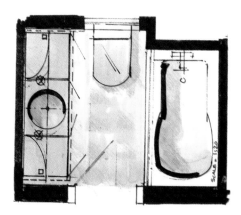

B.

**Figures 3.22A & B** Be creative with color on your drawings; use it on floor plans, elevations and perspectives.

(a. Courtesy of Trudy Summerill, Brighton, Michigan; b. Courtesy of Ines Hanl, Victoria, British Columbia)

Adding color to your drawings is a great way to enhance them. Mastering the use of colored markers and pencils is an art form all its own. Hinting at the color of cabinets and fixtures makes a presentation come to life without being distracting. There are a wide variety of colored markers and pencils from which to choose. When selecting colored pencils, look for soft, heavily-pigmented leads, which give even tones and make blending easy. Markers should always be tested on the paper on which they are to be used, but not the drawing itself, to determine whether they will bleed or cause the lines of the drawing to bleed.

The type of paper used for marker and pencil renderings greatly affects the finished appearance. Markers can be used on almost any type of drafting or art paper. However, vellum is not recommended for use with markers as the ink will not adhere to vellum; instead it puddles on top of the paper and will run. Pencils are recommended for use with vellum. Test any color medium on scrap paper because when colored drawings are reproduced in black and white they may appear muddy or parts of the drawing may be obscured.

**Figure 3.23** An example of a drawing enhanced with colored pencils. (Courtesy of Beth Kemmer, CKD–Fargo, North Dakota)

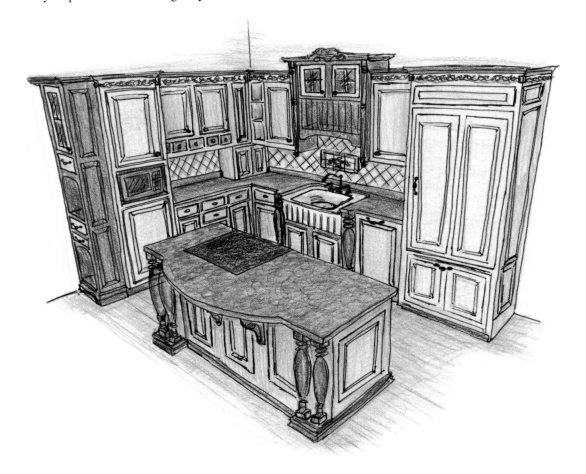

**Figure 3.24** Example of a drawing enhanced with colored markers. (Courtesy of Richard Landon, CMKBD–Bellevue, Washington)

## DRAWING LINES

A drawing consists of three elements: lines, symbols and lettering (or the text on the drawing). Together they illustrate the ideas you have for a client's new kitchen or bathroom. Each of these elements requires practice to become a skilled draftsperson and to develop your own drafting style.

Drafting the lines is step one in putting a design on paper and good line work is critical to the development of a professional drawing presentation. The first lines you draw are called layout lines. As you acquire more experience, you'll spend less time drafting layout lines and move directly to drafting final lines.

To begin, keep lines as light as possible so any changes are easily made and little evidence of those changes shows. You also want to be sure of the placement of the drawing on the paper and the placement of doors and windows. (See Chapter 4 for more information on determining placement.) Regardless of whether the final drawing will be ink or pencil, these first layout lines are drawn with a hard lead, such as a 3H or 4H, because it makes light lines that will be darkened later or virtually invisible once the drawing is complete.

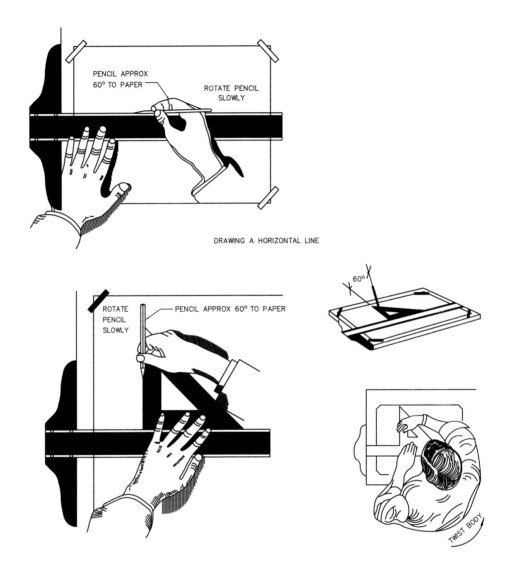

DRAWING A HORIZONTAL LINE

**Figure 3.25** Drawing horizontal and vertical lines.

## Achieving Good Line Work

"Crisp," "uniform" and "precise" are words that characterize good line quality. To achieve pencil lines with these qualities, remember to rotate the pencil between your fingers while drawing and to apply equal pressure throughout the length of the line. Whenever possible, draw a line in a strong, single stroke. To ensure accuracy always keep the pencil sharp. Lines that fade or do not meet at corners will be exaggerated when reproduced and may result in misinterpretation. The final goal of the drafting process is to produce an easily interpreted graphic presentation.

## Types of Lines

Many types of lines are used in one drawing, each representing a unique part of the design.

### VISIBLE OBJECT LINES

Visible object lines are shown with a solid line and indicate objects whose edges are in front of or below the cut-plane and in clear view. In a floor plan, visible object lines are used to show wall cabinets, tall cabinets, countertop surfaces, flooring, furniture, some appliances and any other item not covered or hidden in any way. When cabinets are stacked one above the other, the unit on top takes precedence and is drawn with a solid line. Use a note and arrow to indicate the cabinet at the bottom.

### HIDDEN OBJECT LINES

Hidden object lines represent objects which are under visible objects and are indicated by a series of short dashes. For example, base cabinets are under the countertop so they are drawn with a short dashed line. However, do not indicate hidden features such as a toekick or shelving as they can make the drawing too confusing. Remember how important consistency is; keep the dash length and the spacing between each dash the same. The dashes should be $1/8$-inch long with $1/32$ inch between them to provide a well-proportioned hidden object line.

### OVERHEAD LINES

Overhead lines are indicated by a series of long dashes in the same line weight as object lines. They are used to indicate the edges of any object above the tall cabinets, such as skylights, soffits, extensive molding, etc. Alternate dashes in $1/8$-inch increments to provide a well proportioned overhead line.

**Figure 3.26** Visible and hidden object lines and overhead lines indicate the many items on a drawing.

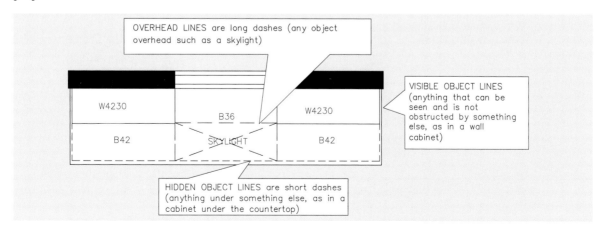

## DIMENSION LINES

Dimension lines are thin, solid lines, which terminate with arrows, dots or slashes. They should be spaced a minimum of $^3/_{16}$ inches apart. Typically, kitchen and bathroom drawings break dimension lines in the middle and the numerical dimension is centered in the opening. This technique used by mechanical draftspersons allows for all numbers to remain vertical and reduces errors caused by misreading the dimension. Equally acceptable, but seen primarily on architectural drawings, is to maintain a solid dimension line and list the numerical dimensions above the line. In this way all dimensions and lettering should be readable from the bottom edge and the right side of the plans.

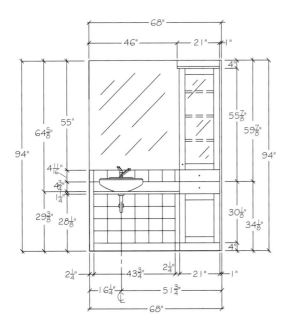

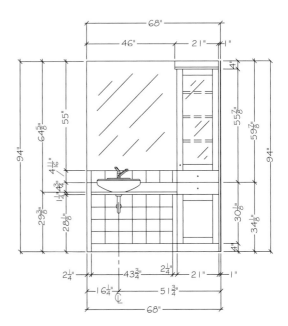

**Figure 3.27** Numerical dimensions. (Courtesy of Sharon Armstrong – St. Petersburg, Florida)

Numerical dimensions should be placed in the open space of their dimension line whenever possible. If the space is too small for both the dimension line and the dimension itself, put only the dimension between the witness lines (defined next). For even smaller spaces, it is acceptable to place the dimension outside of the space with a "leader" indicating the area that is dimensioned.

## WITNESS LINES

Witness lines, also known as extension lines, are used to terminate dimension lines. They are drawn as solid lines, begin approximately $1/16$ inch to $1/8$ inch outside of the object being dimensioned and extend approximately $1/16$ inch to $1/8$ inch beyond the dimension line. They should not touch the walls of the room as they could be interpreted as part of the wall. Indicate the point where witness and dimension lines meet with a dot, arrow or slash. Slashes or "ticks" tilt to the right in horizontal dimensions and to the left in vertical dimensions.

## CENTERLINES

Centerlines are drawn with alternating long and short dashes. The long dashes should be between $3/4$ inch and 1 inch long; the short dashes should be $1/8$ inch long; and the space in between them $1/16$ inch. They should be slightly lighter and thinner than object lines and may extend into the object being located to indicate the exact center of the object. Always start and end a centerline with long dashes. A centerline symbol is used at the end of the line in the dimension line area as illustrated in the drawings in this book.

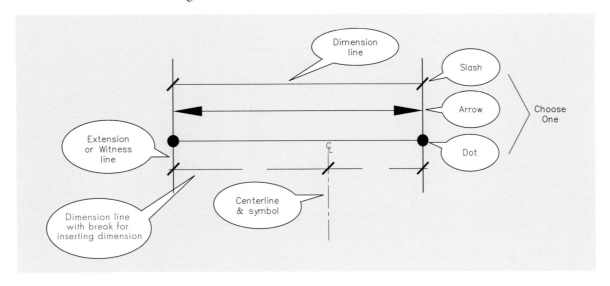

**Figure 3.28** Dimension lines, witness lines, extension lines and centerlines outside the walls of the design indicate the many measurements on the drawing.

## CUTTING PLANE LINES

Cutting plane lines indicate the origin of a section drawing when it is not obvious and are represented by alternating one long dash with two short dashes. They are typically darker and thicker than object lines and terminate with arrows indicating the direction of the section cut. Identification is required in both the plan and elevation views such as A-A or Elevation A. More often kitchen and bathroom plans indicate elevations with a letter and an arrow pointing to the wall without the use of a cutting plane line.

## BREAK LINES

Break lines are indicated by a continuous line interrupted by the break symbol. The line weight is the same as object lines. Use break lines when the entire plan will not fit on the sheet of drafting paper. If the drawing is detailed on both sides of the break line, then two break symbols are required with a blank space between the two symbols. Using break lines and symbols indicates a portion of the drawing has been cut out of the middle. When the drawing is only detailed at one side of the line, the indication is that the drawing continues and only one line is necessary. This will be common in kitchens that are part of a larger great room.

**A.** (Courtesy of Terry Scarborough, Stamford, Connecticut)

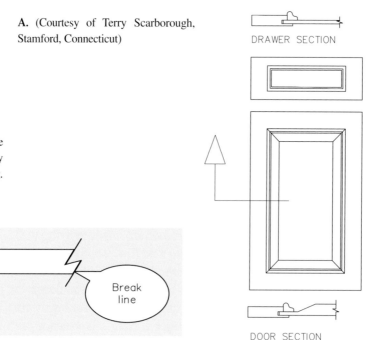

DRAWER SECTION

DOOR SECTION

**Figure 3.29A & B** Both cutting plane lines and break lines are appropriately named as they cut and break the drawing.

**B.**

Break line

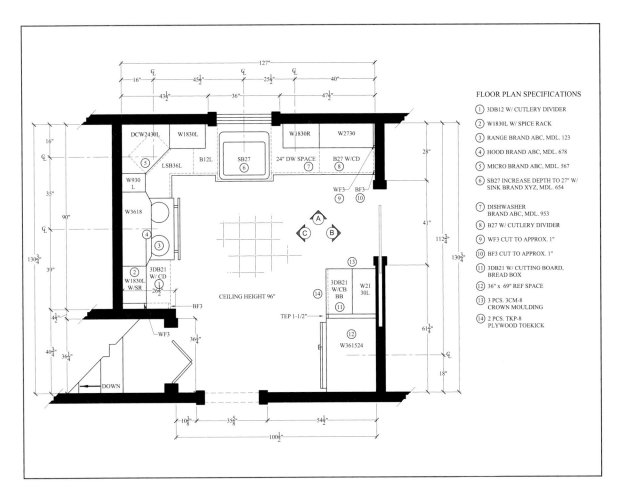

FLOOR PLAN SPECIFICATIONS

1. 3DB12 W/ CUTLERY DIVIDER
2. W1830L W/ SPICE RACK
3. RANGE BRAND ABC, MDL. 123
4. HOOD BRAND ABC, MDL. 678
5. MICRO BRAND ABC, MDL. 567
6. SB27 INCREASE DEPTH TO 27" W/ SINK BRAND XYZ, MDL. 654
7. DISHWASHER BRAND ABC, MDL. 953
8. B27 W/ CUTLERY DIVIDER
9. WF3 CUT TO APPROX. 1"
10. BF3 CUT TO APPROX. 1"
11. 3DB21 W/ CUTTING BOARD, BREAD BOX
12. 36" x 69" REF SPACE
13. 3 PCS. 3CM-8 CROWN MOULDING
14. 2 PCS. TKP-8 PLYWOOD TOEKICK

## SHAPES

Geometric construction may be divided into two categories, simple and complex. The simple elements include points, lines and planes. The complex elements encompass the various solids.

### THE SIMPLE CONSTRUCTION OF SHAPES

All geometric construction begins with a point. Conceptually, a point is without shape, form or dimension. It simply represents a position in space. A point may serve to begin or end a line, mark the intersection of two or more lines, mark a corner when two lines or planes meet, or indicate the center of a field.

**Figure 3.30** Using the different lines in a floor plan. (Concept by Marie Thompson, CKD, CBD–Redmond, Washington)

**Figure 3.31** A point indicates a position in space.

When a point is extended, or two or more points are connected, a line is formed. A line may be straight, curved or angular. A line expresses direction, movement and growth, and dimensional length. As a construction element, a line can join, support, surround, describe an edge or articulate a surface. A straight line may be vertical, horizontal or diagonal.

When a line is manipulated by geometric construction, it may bend, becoming an angle. When a line is formed that connects all the points that are an equal distance from one given point, a circle is formed. A section of a circle is called an arc. Utilizing more complex mathematical formulas, lines can form an ellipse, parabola, hyperbola or various irregular curves.

**Figure 3.32** A drawing is a connection of lines, each serving its own purpose.

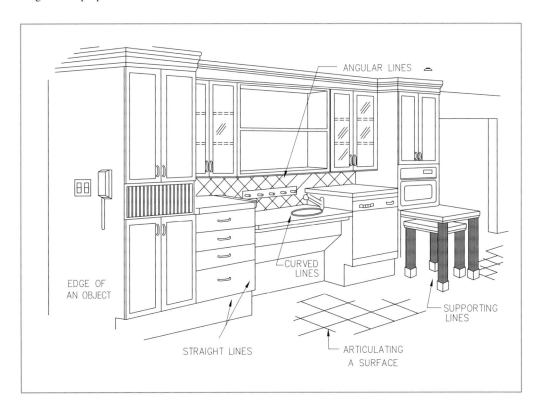

When a line is given width, a plane is created. A plane has dimensional length and width, but no thickness. It may be visualized by comparing it to a piece of rigid paper. The shape of the plane is determined by its linear outline. The plane may take on any curved or angular shape the outline forms.

COMPLEX CONSTRUCTION

The various solid forms which make up the complex elements consists of the cube, cylinder, cone, pyramid, paraboloid and sphere. A solid form possesses length, width and depth, and occupies space in the environment. Solids are mostly comprised of various planes. It is important to understand how solids occupy space so that you can accurately depict them in your drawing.

The most common solid found in design is rectangular and the most simplistic is the cube, comprised of six square planes of equal size enclosing space. A base cabinet is a rectangular form.

**Figure 3.33** Cabinets are the most common solid in a kitchen or bath drawing. (Courtesy of Terry Scarborough, CMKBD–Stamford, Connecticut)

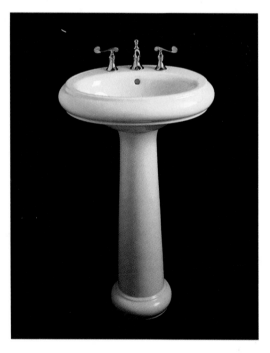

**Figure 3.34** An example of a cylinder in a bathroom is the support of a pedestal sink. (Courtesy of Kohler Company)

A cylinder is formed by two circular planes which are parallel and are connected, creating an enclosed space. A cylindrical form might be a column or support leg for a countertop overhang.

A cone is generated by rotating a triangle about an axis and enclosing it with a circular plane at the bottom. This form may be found in a hanging pendant light fixture.

A pyramid is made entirely of triangular planes. The number of planes is dependent upon how many angles the base has. Some faucet handles have pyramidal forms.

**Figure 3.35** Light fixtures are sometimes cone-shaped. (Courtesy of Task Lighting)

**Figure 3.36** Range hoods are often pyramid shaped. (Courtesy of Sandra Steiner-Houck, CKD–Mechanicsburg, Pennsylvania)

A paraboloid is generated by rotating a parabola about an axis and enclosing it with an ellipse. The curvilinear shape of a contemporary island snack bar would be similar to the paraboloid form.

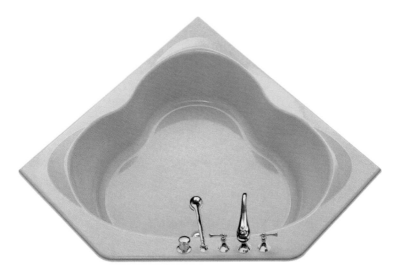

**Figure 3.37** Contemporary designs incorporate the use of paraboloid shapes more than other themes. (Courtesy of Kohler Company)

A sphere retains a circular shape from whatever angle it is viewed. A sphere is defined as an infinite number of points all equidistant from one common point and radiating out in every direction. Perfect spheres are unusual in interiors, but portions of spheres are more commonly seen in faucet handles and lighting fixtures.

A

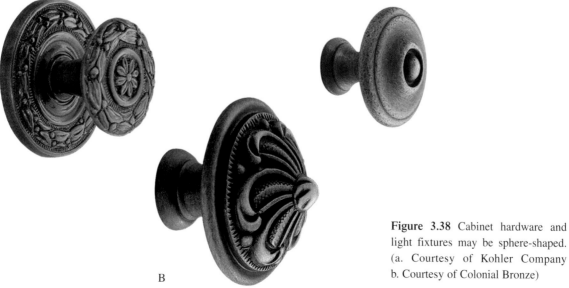

B

**Figure 3.38** Cabinet hardware and light fixtures may be sphere-shaped. (a. Courtesy of Kohler Company b. Courtesy of Colonial Bronze)

## Drawing Parallel Lines

In instances when the floor plan contains an odd angled wall, you may want to repeat the angle elsewhere within the space. To draw this, place any side of your triangle along the given angled line. Move the straight edge in position along the bottom edge of your triangle. Holding the straight edge in place, slide the triangle into the new desired position being sure to keep the bottom edge against the straight edge. Draw your line.

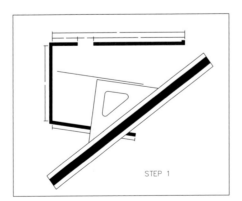
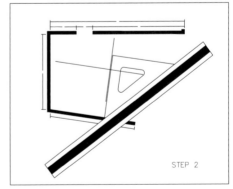

**Figure 3.39** Constructing parallel lines.

## Drawing Perpendicular Lines

Now that you've constructed the parallel line, you'll probably need to draw a perpendicular line through it. Place your straight edge in position with the 45 degree triangle (short side) aligned with the line. Hold the straight edge in place and slide the triangle until it is at the desired place of intersection. Draw a line through the point.

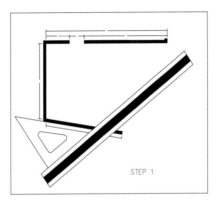
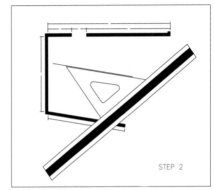

**Figure 3.40** Constructing perpendicular lines.

### Bisecting a Line

To produce symmetrical design drawings you will need to know how to bisect a line. For instance, given a length of wall on which you need to center a sink cabinet, you will first need to bisect the wall line in order to determine its midpoint.

One option is to bisect a line with a compass. Set the compass larger than half the length of the line and draw an arc from each end of the line so that the two arcs intersect each other. The line which passes through the intersecting points of the arcs will bisect the original line.

Another option is to use a straight edge and triangle to bisect a line. Hold the straight edge parallel to the line and draw an equal angle from each end with your triangle toward the center of the line. Then draw a vertical line through the intersection and bisect the original line.

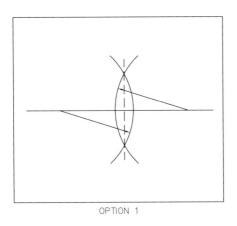

OPTION 1

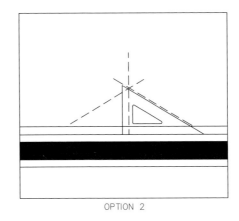

OPTION 2

**Figure 3.41** Bisecting a line.

### Dividing a Line Into Equal Parts

Kitchen drawings often involve decorative tile patterns which need to be illustrated in both floor plan and elevation views. A common illustration might include a 3-inch x 3-inch tile accent stripe between two rows of 12-inch x 12-inch tiles. After the 12-inch tile is drawn, the 3-inch tile lines can be found by dividing the 12-inch length into four equal parts. An easy method for dividing a line equally follows.

Draw a line at any angle from one end of the line to be divided. This line does not have to be the same length as the line to be divided, but rather should be of a length that can be easily divided by the required number of equal parts on the scale being used.

Mark the angled line into equal divisions using your scale. Draw a line from the last mark to the opposite end of the line to be divided. Parallel to that line, draw lines through the remaining marks and through the line to be divided.

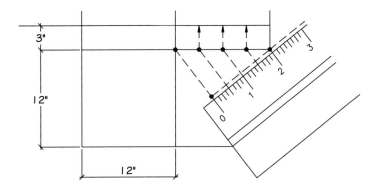

**Figure 3.42** Dividing a line equally.

### Dividing a Space Into Equal Sections

A similar method is used when the space to be divided is between two parallel lines. Find the beginning and end of the number of sections required on your scale. Pivot the scale until it spans the space equally and mark the intermediate points. Draw parallel lines through the points.

This method can be used to draw windows or glass door cabinetry with mullions, or to locate light fixtures evenly within a given amount of space.

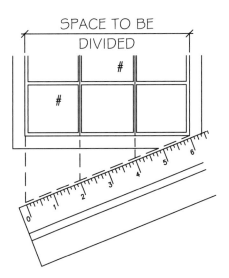

**Figure 3.43** Dividing a space equally.

## Definition of Angles

An angle is formed by the meeting of two lines. How the two lines meet will define the type of angle. The three types of angles are acute, right and obtuse. An acute angle is one that is less than 90°. An angle equal to 90° or with two perpendicular legs is a right angle. Any angle more than 90° is called an obtuse angle.

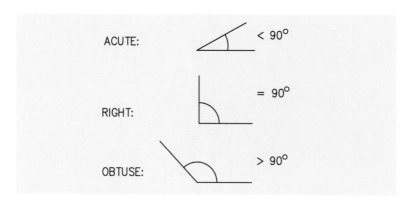

ACUTE:     < 90°

RIGHT:     = 90°

OBTUSE:     > 90°

**Figure 3.44** As a designer, you'll find yourself confronted with angles. Knowing the types will help in the design process.

## Definition of Triangles

Angles are also used to define the types of triangles they create. An acute triangle has three angles each less than 90°. The right triangle has one angle equal to 90° and the obtuse triangle has one angle more than 90°.

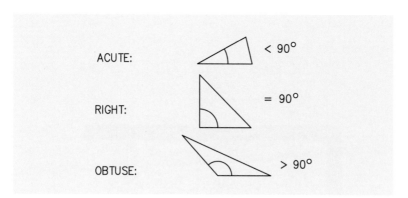

ACUTE:     < 90°

RIGHT:     = 90°

OBTUSE:     > 90°

**Figure 3.45** Triangles have the same names as angles.

You will encounter the right triangle in most angular design situations. To determine the dimensions of cabinetry to be installed on an angle, you'll need to identify the triangles it forms and their side dimensions. First list the known geometric factors; one angle is 90°, one leg of the triangle is equal to the cabinet depth and the two other angles become known based on your choice for placement.

The interior angles will add up to 180°. Therefore, if you are placing a cabinet at a 45° angle, the remaining angle will also be 45°. If you are placing a cabinet at a 30° angle, the remaining angle will be 60°.

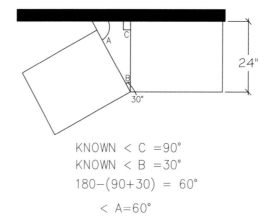

KNOWN < C = 90°
KNOWN < B = 30°
180−(90+30) = 60°
< A = 60°

**Figure 3.46** Identifying the dimensions of cabinetry to be installed on an angle.

To compute the wall space required to place a 30-inch wide desk drawer at a 45° angle in the corner, use the following formula.

**Cw x .7071 = WSa**

**WSa + Cd = TW**

Cw = Cabinet width
Cd = Cabinet depth
WSa = Wall space "a"
TW = Total wall space
.7071 = Formula constant

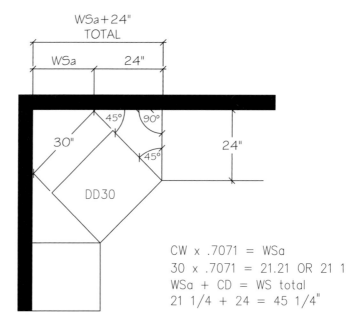

CW x .7071 = WSa
30 x .7071 = 21.21 OR 21 1
WSa + CD = WS total
21 1/4 + 24 = 45 1/4"

**Figure 3.47** Determining the wall space required for a given angled cabinet installation.

## Constructing an Angle Equal to a Given Angle

In new construction, your drawings will often have to be taken from an architect's blueprint. To transfer an odd angle from a blueprint to your own drawing, follow these steps:

1. Draw an arc of any radius from the intersection of the angle on the blueprint.

2. Then draw an arc with the same radius on your drawing.

3. Return to the blueprint. Determine the distance from intersection "x" to intersection "y" with your compass. Draw an arc from intersection "y" through intersection "x."

4. Repeat this process on your own working drawing. Draw the arc through the previous arc you just drew.

5. The point of intersection of the two arcs will also intersect the angle's second leg.

**Figure 3.48** Constructing equal angles in plan view.

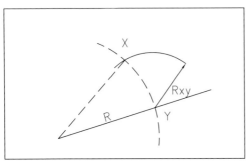

1 — BLUEPRINT

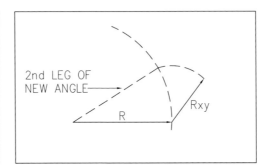

2 — NEW DRAWING

## Constructing Curved Lines With Arcs

Drawing custom countertop plans requires constructing various curved lines.

OPTION 1

1. When the arc is tangent to a right angle, draw an arc with the given radius from the right angle intersection through the two legs.

2. Where the arc intersects the legs, draw another arc inside the right angle from each point so they intersect.

3. From their point of intersection, draw another arc, which will be tangent to the right angle legs.

OPTION 2

1. When the arc is tangent to two lines that are not perpendicular, the arc radius must be an equal distance from each line.

2. Determine the radius center by constructing parallel lines equal distance from each line. Extend these lines until they cross. The point of intersection is the radius location.

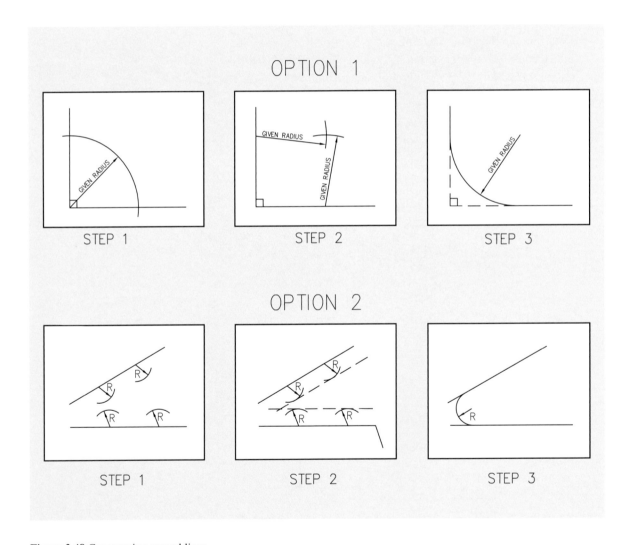

**Figure 3.49** Constructing curved lines with arcs.

## Constructing an Ellipse

You will need to construct an ellipse whenever you draw a perspective that has a circular element in it. Cooktop burners and a vanity sink are good examples of when you might need to draw an ellipse.

OPTION 1

1. First, determine where the widest point or major axis will fall and then where the thinnest point, called the minor axis, will fall.

2. On an edge of a sheet of paper, mark three points A, B and C so that AC equals half the major axis and BC equals half the minor axis.

3. Slide point A up and down along the minor axis while pivoting from the same point and keeping point B on the major axis.

4. Mark several points at C through the process and draw a smooth curve connecting these points.

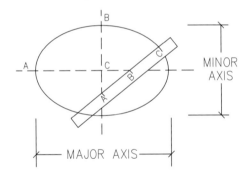

**Figure 3.50** One way to construct an ellipse in plan view.

OPTION 2

An alternative is to sketch a rectangle which will contain the ellipse.

1. Locate the major and minor axis.

2. Divide the rectangle by bisecting the line segments as illustrated in how to bisect a line.

3. Sketch the ellipse to align with the designated points.

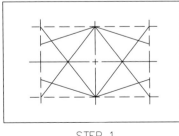

STEP 1

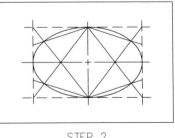

STEP 2

**Figure 3.51** Another way to construct an ellipse in plan view.

## DRWING SYMBOLS

The use of drawing standards is necessary for universal communication within the industry. The following symbols are those most frequently used in kitchen and bathroom drawings.

### Wall Symbols

Typically existing walls are shown $4^1/2$-inches to $6^1/2$-inches thick in $^1/2$-inch scale and filled in with black ink or pencil; half walls are not filled in. However, because filling in the opening by hand is very time consuming, hollow walls are accepted in this industry. Be sure to note any walls that are not full height if you choose this method.

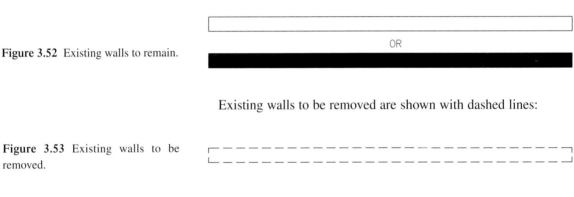

**Figure 3.52** Existing walls to remain.

Existing walls to be removed are shown with dashed lines:

**Figure 3.53** Existing walls to be removed.

Existing openings to be enclosed are filled in with several parallel lines:

**Figure 3.54** Existing openings to be enclosed.

Newly constructed walls should indicate the type of material used in construction in the form of a note or a symbol identified in the legend:

**Figure 3.55** New walls to be constructed.

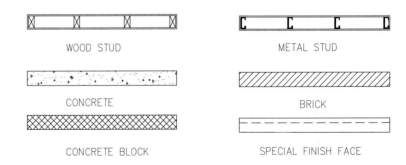

## Door Symbols

Doors should always indicate open or cased framing and the direction of swing. In most instances, a 45° swing is acceptable. If there are any questions as to clearance, a 90° swing should be shown. A door schedule is only required with new doors and is indicated by a letter in a circle inside each door opening. If there is only one new door, the schedule information can be indicated directly within the floor plan in note form. There are several types of doors. The illustration shows the symbols of ones typically used on kitchen and bathroom drawings.

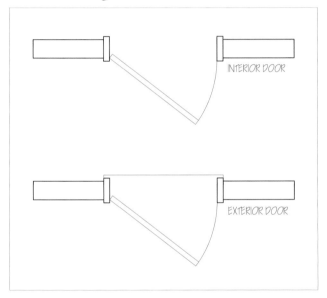

INTERIOR DOOR

EXTERIOR DOOR

**Figure 3.56** The illustrations show typically used door symbols on kitchen and bath drawings. (Continued on next page.)

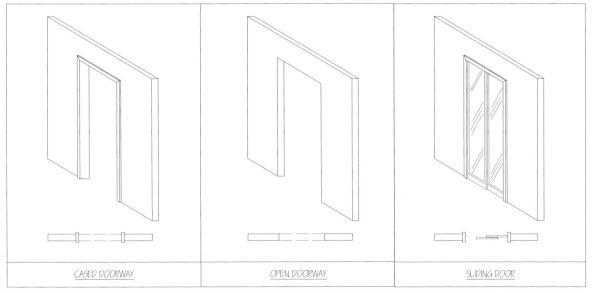

CASED DOORWAY

OPEN DOORWAY

SLIDING DOOR

## Door Symbols continued

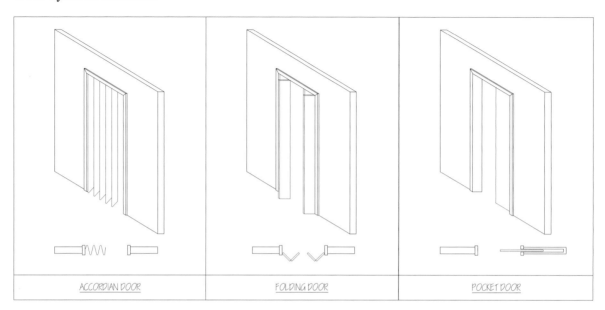

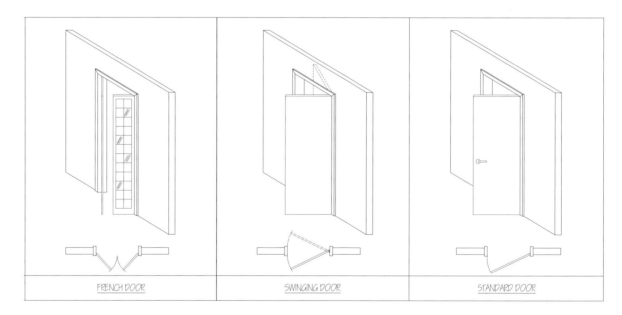

## Window Symbols

Window symbols should always indicate open or cased framing. However, window sills are typically not shown unless a particular interior treatment is to be used. If the window is a casement style, the indication of the glass swing direction is optional and if shown, should be of short dashes. Glass block is shown as a series of squares or rectangles with a listing in the specifications. Skylights are shown using overhead lines and are labeled inside the symbol. Pertinent information is referenced at the side.

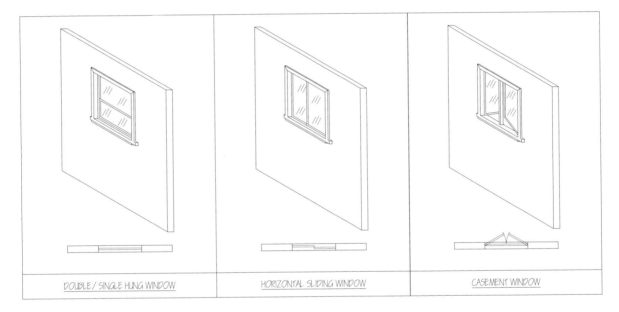

DOUBLE / SINGLE HUNG WINDOW        HORIZONTAL SLIDING WINDOW        CASEMENT WINDOW

**Figure 3.57** Window and glass block symbols. (Continued on next page.)

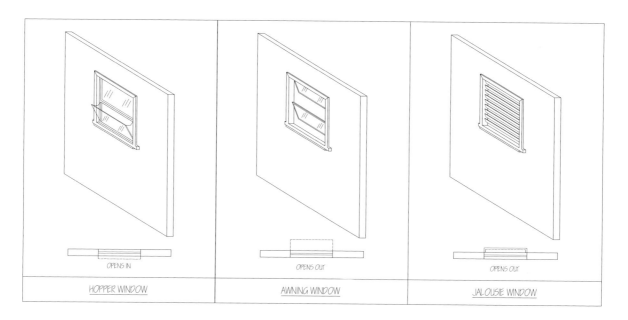

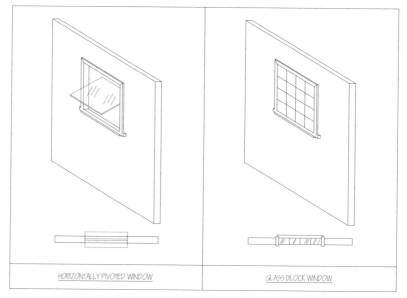

## Stair and Ramp Symbols

The way to show stairs is to draw the treads with a directional arrow and the word "UP" at the beginning of the stairs. If the design incorporates the other floor, the total number of risers should be indicated. Otherwise it is acceptable to show a partial set of stairs or ramp by using a break line. Indicate the direction of the slope with an arrow leading from the main floor area to the secondary area and the word "UP" or "DOWN."

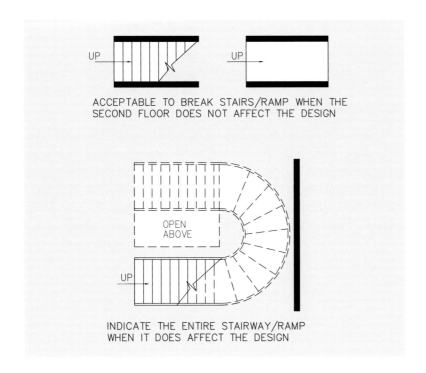

ACCEPTABLE TO BREAK STAIRS/RAMP WHEN THE SECOND FLOOR DOES NOT AFFECT THE DESIGN

INDICATE THE ENTIRE STAIRWAY/RAMP WHEN IT DOES AFFECT THE DESIGN

**Figure 3.58** Stair and ramp symbols.

## Elevator Symbols

Elevators and hydraulic lifts are indicated with an "x" inside of the outline of the interior size. The "x" is used to indicate that the unit runs through the entire space beyond the floor and/or ceiling. Include the appropriate door symbol to show the elevator opening.

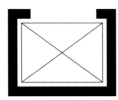

ADD APPROPRIATE DOOR SYMBOL TO ELEVATORS AND LIFTS

**Figure 3.59** Elevator symbol.

## Kitchen Appliance and Bathroom Fixture Symbols

Symbols for kitchen appliances and equipment and bathroom fixtures should remain consistent throughout the set of drawings. Faucet and tub filler locations should always be indicated on the floor plan and mechanical plan.

Kitchen appliance doors and handles are simply shown as thick solid lines. They may be labeled within the floor plan but some designers prefer to number them with an adjacent schedule to eliminate a cluttered drawing. It is optional to indicate door swings with a dotted line. Showing the door swing may be important if the design calls for several appliances to be placed in a work aisle or traffic path.

**Figure 3.60** Typical symbols for kitchen appliances and equipment.

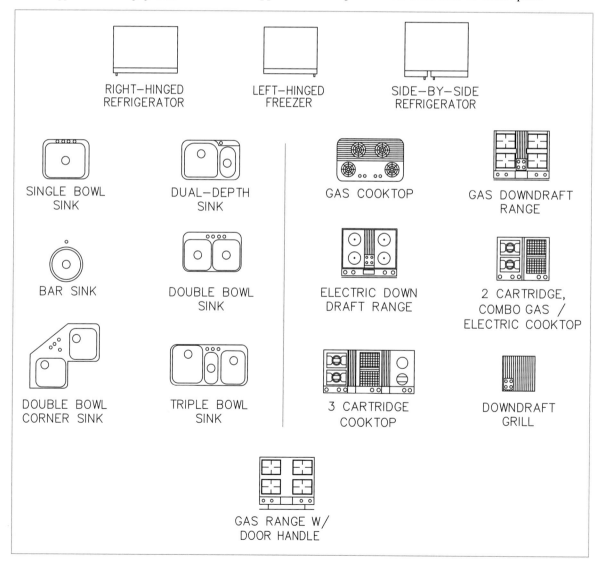

**Figure 3.61** Typical symbols for bathroom fixtures.

**Figure 3.62** Handrail, grab bar or towel bar symbol.

Interior or exterior handrails, grab bars and towel bars are all shown with double solid lines. Use a one- or two-word description near the symbol directly within the drawing if it does not make the drawing too cluttered. However, numbering the symbol and listing it in the specifications or schedule is equally acceptable.

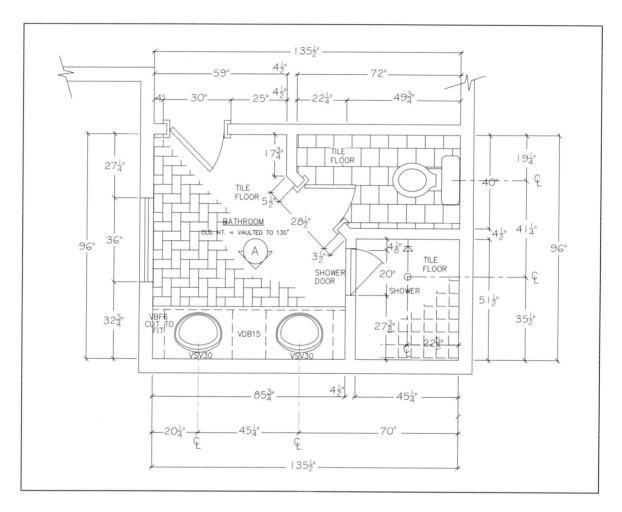

**Figure 3.63** Examples of symbols for finished flooring materials. (Courtesy of Simone Feldman, CKD, CBD–Atlanta, Georgia)

It is preferred to indicate a sample of the decking and flooring materials in a blank area of the drawing rather than the entire space. However, if the drawing does not allow for a clear indication, it is better not to show any. Be sure to include them in the specifications either way.

## MECHANICAL SYMBOLS

For the purpose of kitchen and bathroom mechanical plans, the mechanical symbols used indicate lighting, electrical, plumbing, heating and ventilation. The accuracy of illustrating these particular symbols is very important because the professional tradesperson must be able to interpret your drawing. Even though these symbols are generally universal, include a legend on your mechanical plan to eliminate any questions. This list is extensive, but it is possible that a symbol does not exist for a specific item. In that case it is acceptable to create a symbol of your own, as long as you list it and describe it in the specifications. The following pages include mechanical symbols seen on most kitchen and bath drawings. Next to each symbol is a description and picture of the item.

The majority of the symbols found in the following pages are consistent with the Architectural Graphic Standards Manual (American Institute of Architects). However, some symbols may be unique to NKBA to keep up with changes to the products that kitchen and bath designers must specify. For the purpose of kitchen and bathroom mechanical plans, the mechanical symbols used indicate lighting, electrical, plumbing, heating and ventilation. Occasionally, the designer will encounter a product and may not be sure of the correct symbol. If a resource fails to provide you with the correct symbol, you may need to create your own. When creating a symbol, you must describe it in the mechanical plan legend. Do not take this statement as permission to develop your own set of mechanical symbols.

## Switch Symbols

| SYMBOL | APPEARANCE | NOTES | SYMBOL | APPEARANCE | NOTES |
|---|---|---|---|---|---|
| S | | SINGLE POLE SWITCH<br>ACTIVATES ONE OR MORE LIGHTS OR FIXTURES FROM ONE LOCATION. | S$_D$ | | DOOR SWITCH<br>ACTIVATES LIGHTS OR FIXTURES BEHIND DOOR WHEN DOOR IS OPENED. USED FOR PANTRY OR CLOSET. |
| S$_3$ | | 3-WAY SWITCH<br>ACTIVATES ONE OR MORE LIGHTS OR FIXTURES FROM TWO LOCATIONS. REQUIRED FOR ROOMS WITH TWO ENTRANCES. | S$_P$ | | SWITCH W/ PILOT LIGHT<br>PILOT LIGHT IS LIT WHEN SWITCH IS IN THE ON POSITION. USED FOR BASEMENT, ATTIC AND GARAGE LIGHTS. |
| S$_4$ | | 4-WAY SWITCH<br>USED WITH TWO 3-WAY SWITCHES TO ACTIVATE ONE OR MORE LIGHTS OR FIXTURES FROM THREE LOCATIONS. | S<br>SIDE VIEW | | CEILING PULL SWITCH<br>PORCELAIN LIGHT FIXTURE WITH PULL CHAIN TO ACTIVATE LIGHT. IDEAL FOR ATTICS, CRAWL SPACES, ETC. |
| SSS | | THREE SWITCHES AT ONE LOCATION. THREE SINGLE POLE SWITCHES IN A THREE GANG BOX ILLUSTRATED. | S$_2$ | | DOUBLE POLE SWITCH<br>SELDOM USED IN THE HOME. NORMALLY USED FOR 240-VOLT APPLIANCES THAT ARE SWITCHED. CAN BE CONFUSED WITH A 4-WAY SWITCH, BUT IS MARKED ON AND OFF. |
| S$_{DM}$ | | DIMMER SWITCH<br>USED TO CONTROL THE INTENSITY OF ONE OR MORE LIGHTS FROM ONE LOCATION. ROTATES FROM OFF TO FULL ON. OTHER TYPES OF DIMMER SWITCHES WILL USE THIS SAME SYMBOL. | S$_K$ | | KEY SWITCH<br>SELDOM USED IN THE HOME. A KEY MUST BE USED TO ACTIVATE THE SWITCH. OFTEN USED IN PUBLIC SPACES SUCH AS PUBLIC RESTROOMS. |
| S$_{3DM}$ | | THREE-WAY DIMMER SWITCH<br>SAME AS ABOVE BUT USED TO CONTROL LIGHTS FROM TWO LOCATIONS. ONLY ONE OF THE THREE-WAY SWITCHES CAN BE THE DIMMER SWITCH. | T$_*$ | | ELECTRIC THERMOSTAT<br>WALL MOUNTED UNIT TO CONTROL ROOM OR HOME TEMPERATURE.<br>* INDICATE TYPE:<br>  C - COOLING<br>  H - HEATING<br>  C/H - COOLING/HEATING |
| S<br>S<br>S | | THREE SWITCHES STACKED AT ONE LOCATION. TYPICALLY USED FOR BATHROOM VENTILATION UNITS. | H | | HUMIDISTAT<br>CAN BE PRE-SET TO TURN BATHROOM FAN ON AUTOMATICALLY WHEN THE HUMIDITY REACHES A SET LEVEL. |

**Figure 3.64** Switch symbols.

## Receptacle Symbols

| SYMBOL | NOTES | SYMBOL | NOTES |
|---|---|---|---|
| **120-VOLT** <br> * HEIGHT <br> * TYPE <br> * HEIGHT <br> * TYPE | **HEIGHT** <br> INDICATE HEIGHT THAT IS NOT STANDARD. AS AN EXAMPLE, 42" AFF WILL INDICATE THE BOX IS TO BE PLACED 42" ABOVE THE FINISHED FLOOR RATHER THAN THE STANDARD HEIGHT OF APPROXIMATELY 12" - 18". | _S | **DUPLEX RECEPTACLE W/ SWITCH** <br> DUPLEX RECEPTACLE MOUNTED ADJACENT TO A SINGLE POLE SWITCH IN A TWO-GANG BOX. |
| **240-VOLT** <br> * HEIGHT <br> * TYPE | **TYPE** <br> INDICATE TYPE OF RECEPTACLE. <br><br> **120-VOLT EXAMPLES** <br> CW - CLOTHES WASHER <br> DW - DISHWASHER <br> GRI - GROUND FAULT INTERRUPT <br> MW - MICROWAVE <br> R - REFRIGERATOR <br> WP - WATERPROOF <br><br> **240-VOLT EXAMPLES** <br> AC - AIR CONDITIONER <br> CD - CLOTHES DRYER <br> EH - ELECTRIC HEATER <br> R - RANGE <br> S - SAUNA <br> WP - WHIRLPOOL TUB | C | **CLOCK RECEPTACLE** <br> THE RECEPTACLE AREA IS RECESSED TO ALLOW THE CLOCK TO FIT FLUSH WITH THE WALL. |
| | **SINGLE RECEPTACLE** <br> NORMALLY USED FOR AN APPLIANCE OR FIXTURE REQUIRING A DEDICATED CIRCUIT. | | **SPLIT-WIRED DUPLEX RECEPTACLE** <br> A SIDE VIEW SHOWS HOW THE TOP AND BOTTOM CAN BE SEPARATED SO THE TOP CAN BE CONTROLLED WITH A SWITCH WHILE THE BOTTOM IS ALWAYS "HOT." GREAT FOR A BEDSIDE LAMP AND CLOCK RADIO. |
| | **DOUBLE RECEPTACLE** <br> STANDARD DUPLEX GROUNDED RECEPTACLE. | WP | **WATERPROOF RECEPTACLE** <br> DUPLEX RECEPTACLE WITH WATERPROOF COVER. |
| | **QUADRUPLEX RECEPTACLE** <br> FOUR RECEPTACLES IN A TWO-GANG BOX. | | **SINGLE FLOOR RECEPTACLE** <br> A METAL PLATE WITH SCREW-OFF CAP COVERS THE SINGLE RECEPTACLE. INDICATE HEIGHT IF NOT AT FLOOR LEVEL. |
| | **TRIPLEX RECEPTACLE** <br> THREE RECEPTACLES IN A TWO-GANG BOX. | | **DUPLEX FLOOR RECEPTACLE** <br> A METAL PLATE WITH SCREW-OFF CAP COVERS THE DUPLEX RECEPTACLE. INDICATE HEIGHT IF NOT AT FLOOR LEVEL. |

**Figure 3.65A** Receptacle symbols.

## Receptacle Symbols Continued

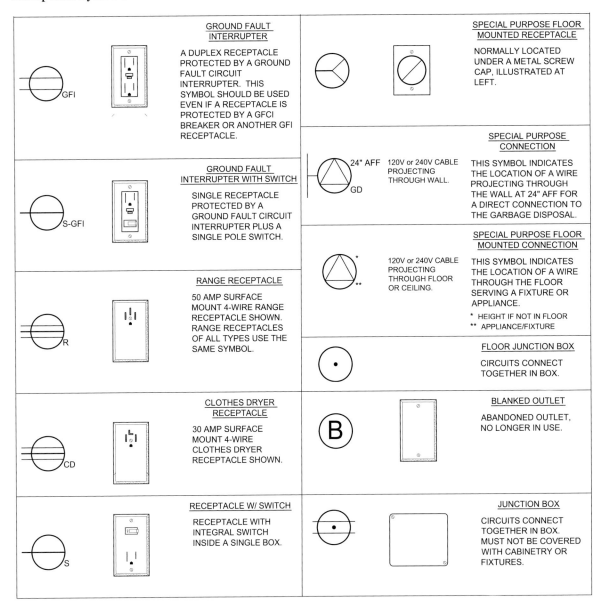

**GROUND FAULT INTERRUPTER**

A DUPLEX RECEPTACLE PROTECTED BY A GROUND FAULT CIRCUIT INTERRUPTER. THIS SYMBOL SHOULD BE USED EVEN IF A RECEPTACLE IS PROTECTED BY A GFCI BREAKER OR ANOTHER GFI RECEPTACLE.

**GROUND FAULT INTERRUPTER WITH SWITCH**

SINGLE RECEPTACLE PROTECTED BY A GROUND FAULT CIRCUIT INTERRUPTER PLUS A SINGLE POLE SWITCH.

**RANGE RECEPTACLE**

50 AMP SURFACE MOUNT 4-WIRE RANGE RECEPTACLE SHOWN. RANGE RECEPTACLES OF ALL TYPES USE THE SAME SYMBOL.

**CLOTHES DRYER RECEPTACLE**

30 AMP SURFACE MOUNT 4-WIRE CLOTHES DRYER RECEPTACLE SHOWN.

**RECEPTACLE W/ SWITCH**

RECEPTACLE WITH INTEGRAL SWITCH INSIDE A SINGLE BOX.

**SPECIAL PURPOSE FLOOR MOUNTED RECEPTACLE**

NORMALLY LOCATED UNDER A METAL SCREW CAP, ILLUSTRATED AT LEFT.

**SPECIAL PURPOSE CONNECTION**

24" AFF   120V or 240V CABLE PROJECTING THROUGH WALL.

THIS SYMBOL INDICATES THE LOCATION OF A WIRE PROJECTING THROUGH THE WALL AT 24" AFF FOR A DIRECT CONNECTION TO THE GARBAGE DISPOSAL.

**SPECIAL PURPOSE FLOOR MOUNTED CONNECTION**

120V or 240V CABLE PROJECTING THROUGH FLOOR OR CEILING.

THIS SYMBOL INDICATES THE LOCATION OF A WIRE THROUGH THE FLOOR SERVING A FIXTURE OR APPLIANCE.

\* HEIGHT IF NOT IN FLOOR
\*\* APPLIANCE/FIXTURE

**FLOOR JUNCTION BOX**

CIRCUITS CONNECT TOGETHER IN BOX.

**BLANKED OUTLET**

ABANDONED OUTLET, NO LONGER IN USE.

**JUNCTION BOX**

CIRCUITS CONNECT TOGETHER IN BOX. MUST NOT BE COVERED WITH CABINETRY OR FIXTURES.

**Figure 3.65B** Receptacle symbols.

## Lighting Symbols

| SYMBOL | NOTES | SYMBOL | NOTES |
|---|---|---|---|
| 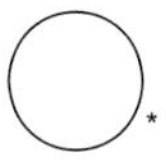 CEILING MOUNT | IDENTIFYING TYPES OF LIGHTING<br><br>* SINCE LIGHT FIXTURES CAN HOLD DIFFERENT LAMPS, YOU MUST NOTE THE TYPE OF LAMP YOU SUGGEST. USE THE FOLLOWING TO IDENTIFY THE FIXTURE.<br><br>FL — FLUORESCENT LAMP<br>HA — HALOGEN LAMP<br>IN — INANDESCENT LAMP | CEILING MOUNTED SPOTLIGHT<br><br>INDICATE TYPE OF LIGHTING. ARROW INDICATES DIRECTION OF FOCUS. |
| 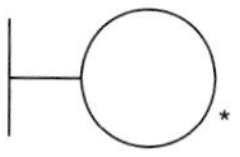 WALL MOUNT | EXAMPLE 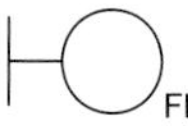<br><br>A WALL HUNG FIXTURE WITH A FLUORESCENT LAMP.<br>FL | CEILING MOUNTED LIGHT TRACK<br><br>INDICATE TYPE OF LIGHTING. SHOW NUMBER OF FIXTURES REQUIRED. |
| SIDE VIEW OF CEILING MOUNTED FIXTURE | CEILING MOUNTED LIGHT FIXTURE<br><br>INDICATE TYPE OF LIGHTING. | RECESSED FIXTURE FOR DAMP LOCATION<br><br>FIXTURE IS DESIGN FOR DAMP USE SUCH AS SHOWERS.<br><br>* NOTE TYPE OF LAMP. |
| | CEILING MOUNTED WALL-WASHER FIXTURE<br><br>INDICATE TYPE OF LIGHTING. SHADING INDICATES LIGHTED FACE. | CEILING MOUNTED FLUORESCENT FIXTURE<br><br>INDICATE TYPE. DRAW TO SCALE. |
| | RECESSED FIXTURE<br><br>RECESSED CEILING FIXTURE.<br><br>* NOTE TYPE OF LAMP. | FLUORESCENT STRIP LIGHT<br><br>INDICATE TYPE. DRAW TO SCALE. |
| | | SURFACE MOUNTED (VERTICAL) FLUORESCENT<br><br>VERTICAL LINE INDICATES WALL MOUNTING. CAN NOT BE SCALED ON MECHANICAL PLAN. |
| | HANGING FIXTURE<br><br>HANGING CEILING FIXTURE.<br><br>* NOTE TYPE OF LAMP. | 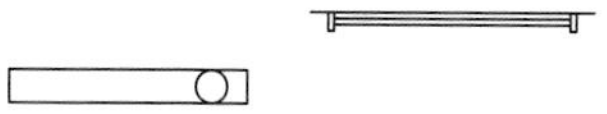 8' CEILING MOUNTED FIXTURE ILLUSTRATED — SURFACE MOUNTED (VERTICAL) FLUORESCENT<br><br>VERTICAL LINE INDICATES WALL MOUNTING. CAN NOT BE SCALED ON MECHANICAL PLAN. |

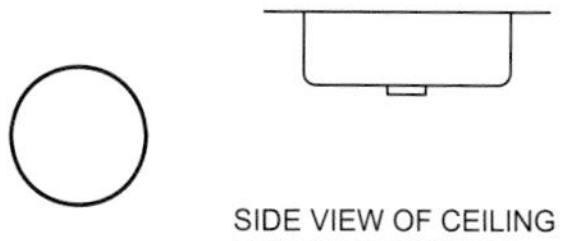

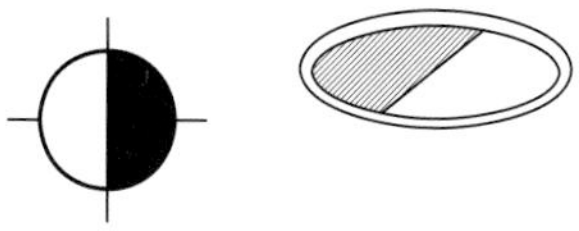

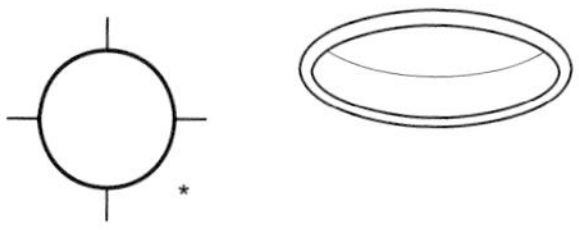

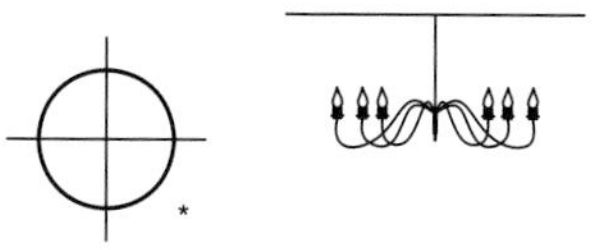

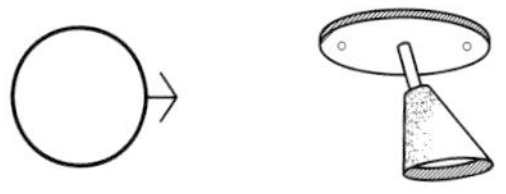

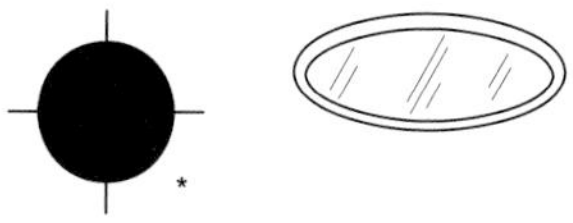

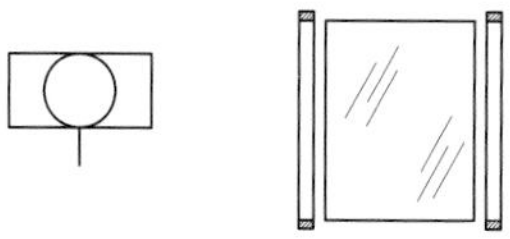

**Figure 3.66** Lighting symbols.

## Communication Symbols

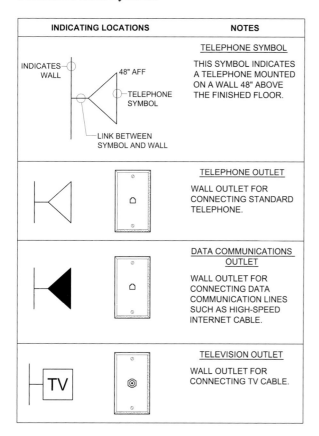

**Figure 3.67** Communication symbols.

## Miscellaneous Symbols

| SYMBOL | NOTES |
|---|---|
| F | **FAN HANGER OUTLET**<br>THIS SYMBOL INDICATES AN OUTLET BOX THAT IS REINFORCED TO SUPPORT A FAN.  SINCE THERE IS NO VERTICAL LINE TO INDICATE A WALL OR A LINK FROM THE SYMBOL TO THE WALL, THE SYMBOL INDICATES EITHER FLOOR OR CEILING MOUNT. |

| SYMBOL | APPEARANCE | NOTES |
|---|---|---|
| S |  | **SMOKE DETECTOR**<br>SYMBOL INDICATES CEILING MOUNT. |

| | |
|---|---|
| W.H. | WATER HEATER |

**RADIATOR OR CONVECTOR SYMBOLS**

(WALL)    FREE STANDING
RAD

RAD    RECESSED

RAD    RECESSED WITH ENCLOSURE

**Figure 3.68** Miscellaneous symbols.

## THE IMPORTANCE OF GOOD LETTERING

A drawing relies on lettering to convey information that is not graphically obvious: identification, titles, dimensions, nomenclature, specifications and notes. Good lettering enhances the appearance and more importantly, the clarity of the drawing.

By contrast, poor lettering is difficult to read and detracts from the drawing. Consistency is the most important element in good lettering. However, consistency is not the only element; legibility is a very close second. Even if your design is award-winning, you need to communicate much of it through the words on the drawings. Everyone who needs to use the drawings to install the room will have a difficult time if the words are illegible. In complex designs, where many notes are required to communicate the ideas, consistent and legible lettering is vital.

Freehand lettering is generally preferred on design drawings but is an acquired skill. After considerable experience, freehand lettering takes on an individual style that frequently enhances the presentation. Your personal lettering style will develop from practicing the Gothic alphabet discussed in this chapter. However, be cautious not to get so stylized that legibility is compromised.

Mechanical tools may be used until you are comfortable lettering freehand. Notes can be typed on clear adhesive-backed film, cut and applied directly to the drawing. Or use a lettering template. Templates are available for various lettering sizes. These control consistency in letter size and shape, but you are responsible for placement.

### Developing a Lettering Style

The Gothic alphabet, which uses all capital letters, is the base from which the standard "single stroke" lettering technique has evolved. This technique has acquired universal acceptance because it is easy to read and easily executed. Keep in mind that the same lettering style should be used throughout the drawing presentation. Slanted lettering should be avoided because it is directional and suggests movement which will detract from your plans. Keep lettering vertical and maintain an oblong proportion. Master the vertical, single-stroke lettering technique illustrated before developing an individual style.

There are five basic elements which aid in letter consistency: height, form, direction, weight and spacing.

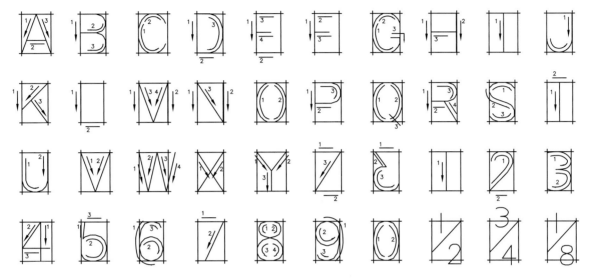

**Figure 3.69** Follow this technique to develop skillful lettering.

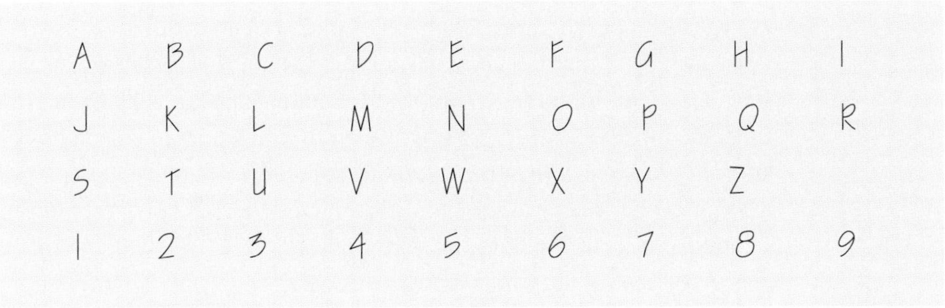

| A | B | C | D | E | F | G | H | I |
| J | K | L | M | N | O | P | Q | R |
| S | T | U | V | W | X | Y | Z |
| 1 | 2 | 3 | 4 | 5 | 6 | 7 | 8 | 9 |

**Figure 3.70** A sample of hand-drafted lettering.

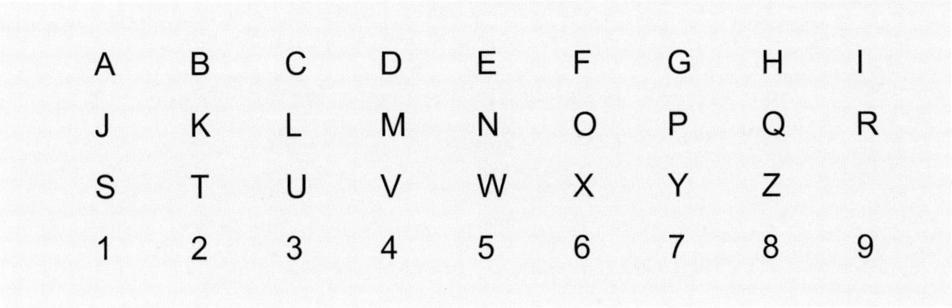

| A | B | C | D | E | F | G | H | I |
| J | K | L | M | N | O | P | Q | R |
| S | T | U | V | W | X | Y | Z |
| 1 | 2 | 3 | 4 | 5 | 6 | 7 | 8 | 9 |

**Figure 3.71** A sample of computer lettering.

Consistent height of lettering and spacing between rows of lettering requires guide lines. It is nearly impossible to maintain straight horizontal lettering without the use of guide lines. On inked drawings, guide lines will be erased. On pencil drawings, they will remain. Therefore, guide lines should be drawn with a sharp point and a light touch. A lettering guide helps maintain even spacing of the lines.

To determine the amount of space required between rows of lettering, consider the size of the lettering and the number of rows of lettering. Generally, the space between rows of lettering is slightly smaller than the letter size. However, for small, lengthy notes, the space should be equal to the letter size to ensure legibility. Therefore make sure the letters terminate at the exact top and bottom of each guide line. When using a technical ink pen, achieve the same effect by making slow and deliberate strokes and holding the pen point on the paper slightly longer at the start and end of each stroke.

Legibility also depends on consistent spacing. Letter spacing is not based on actual equal spaces, but rather perceived equal spaces. Each letter of the alphabet has a different shape; therefore, the letters must be visually spaced rather than measured. Letters with two vertical adjacent edges require more visual space than do angled or curved letters. A helpful hint is to squint. If the letters appear as an even gray tone, then the spaces are even. However, if you squint and see gaps or varying gray tones, then the letters are perceived as unevenly spaced. The space between words should be larger than the space between individual letters. For an attractive plan, try to leave twice as much space between words than between letters, and leave slightly more space between sentences than between words.

Form refers to the vertical, horizontal and curvilinear lines of each letter and how they relate to each other. Each straight line or curve should appear the same. Good form simply comes from practice.

**Figure 3.72** Using a lettering guide like the one illustrated helps to create straight horizontal lettering. (Courtesy of Alvin & Co., Inc.)

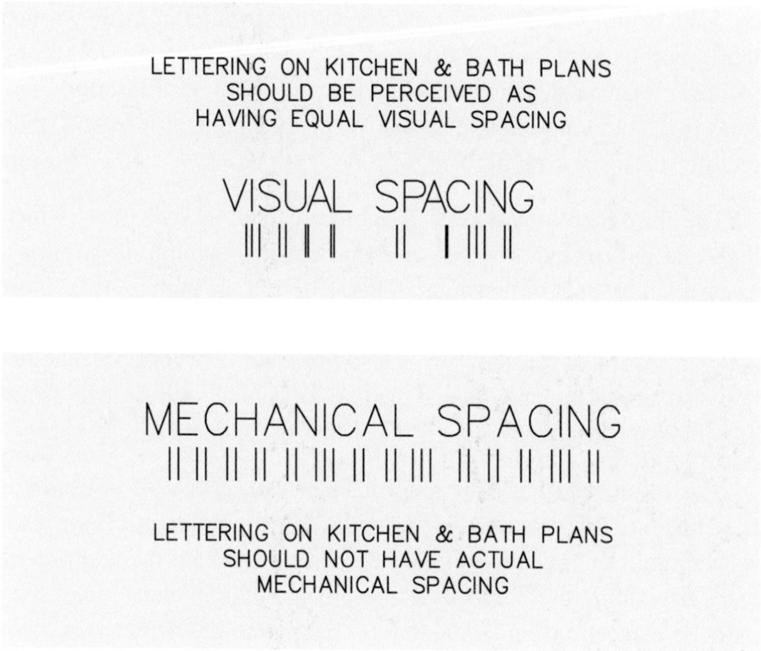

LETTERING ON KITCHEN & BATH PLANS
SHOULD BE PERCEIVED AS
HAVING EQUAL VISUAL SPACING

VISUAL SPACING
||| || | | ||   ||   | ||| ||

MECHANICAL SPACING
|| || || || || ||| || || ||| || || || || ||| ||

LETTERING ON KITCHEN & BATH PLANS
SHOULD NOT HAVE ACTUAL
MECHANICAL SPACING

**Figure 3.73** The space between letters and words is visual, not mechanical.

Whenever possible, strokes should be made by pulling the pencil/pen across the paper, not pushing it. Generally a right-handed draftsperson will pull down and to the right. If needed, a small triangle can be used as a quick and efficient way to make vertical strokes.

Good line weight is also developed with practice. The lettering on a drawing should be informative not distracting, crisp and sharp, not heavy and bold, but dark enough to be seen when photocopied. For lettering on pencil drawings, a 2H or 3H lead is recommended depending on the pressure you exert on the pencil. Rotate the pencil to keep a consistent point width and even line widths. Emphasize the start and end of each stroke by applying slightly more pressure.

### The Four Lettering Sizes

The most general information is shown with the largest lettering, and the most detailed and specific information appears in the smallest lettering. It is important to remain consistent in each lettering size category to ensure a professional, standardized drawing presentation. Typically, no lettering is larger than $1/2$ inch and none is smaller than $1/8$ inch.

The first size is also the largest at $1/2$ inch and will demand the most skill in composition and spacing because of the longer strokes that make up each letter. The title block lettering is included in this first category.

Titles within the drawing rank second in size hierarchy at $^1/4$-inch high. For example on a floor plan drawing, the title might be "Kitchen". On an elevation drawing, the title might be "Elevation View A1". If the drawing includes a list of specifications or a legend, then its title is also $^1/4$-inch high.

The third size of lettering is approximately $^1/8$-inch to $^3/16$-inch high and will include the list of specifications, symbol descriptions, nomenclature and dimensions. This lettering is perhaps the most important category since these things describe specific pieces in the space. Location of this lettering is also important. For instance, cabinet nomenclature is typically inside the lines of cabinets where there is not a lot of room for lengthy text or large letters and numbers.

The fourth and smallest lettering size on a drawing is used for specific notes to explain drawing details. For example, on a floor plan, special areas of construction may be obscure without the addition of notes explaining the detailed design process. On an elevation, a note may be needed to indicate that a particular drawerhead is "not operable." To eliminate possible confusion, use notes only when needed. To guarantee readability, hand lettering should never be any smaller than $^1/8$-inch.

**Figure 3.74** The four lettering sizes.

# Chapter 4: Prepare the Drawings —
# The Steps of Hand Drafting

To begin the drafting process, assemble your equipment, sketches and rough drawings within reach around your drawing board. Set your board at a comfortable incline (approximately 10° to 15°). The incline helps ensure accuracy by enabling you to see above the equipment, as well as reduces back strain caused by bending over your work. Now you are ready to begin drawing a floor plan.

As a reminder, every floor plan should show as a minimum

- Overall length of wall areas to receive cabinets, countertops, fixtures, or any equipment occupying floor and/or wall space

- Each wall opening (windows, arches, and doors), major appliances and fixed structures (chimneys, protrusions and partitions) individually dimensioned from outside trim

- Trim size noted in the specification list

- Fixtures such as radiators remaining in place

- Ceiling heights

- Additional notes for any deviation from standard height, width and depth (cabinets, countertops, etc.)

- The exact height, width and depth for areas to be left open to receive equipment, cabinets, appliances and fixtures at a future date.

**10 STEPS TO DRAWING
A FLOOR PLAN**

**Figure 4.1** Align paper edge or borderline with straight edges. (Courtesy of NKBA)

**Step 1:** Tape your paper down to the board using drafting tape or dots. It is important to line it up with your straight edge to make sure the drawing will be square on the sheet of paper. If the paper has a preprinted border, align the border with your straight edge and then tape the paper in place. If there is no border, then align the edge of the paper with the straight edge.

**Step 2:** Visualize the finished drawing. Remember, you are drawing in a scale of $^1/2$ inch equals one foot (1' 0") or 12 inches. All dimensions will be noted in inches.

Decide if you will list the specifications at the right side or at the bottom. Also allow room for a title. Roughly estimate how big your drawing will be so you know how much space it will take up on the paper. Do not forget to include space for the dimension lines. Now determine where to locate the drawing on the paper. One way is to start in the center of the space that remains after allowing room for the specs and title. If more than one drawing will appear on the same sheet, block out the separate areas with light pencil outlines.

**Step 3:** Begin by lightly penciling in all of the walls. By drawing all of the walls in first, any mistakes caused by incorrect scaling or measuring will be caught before too much time is spent drawing in details.

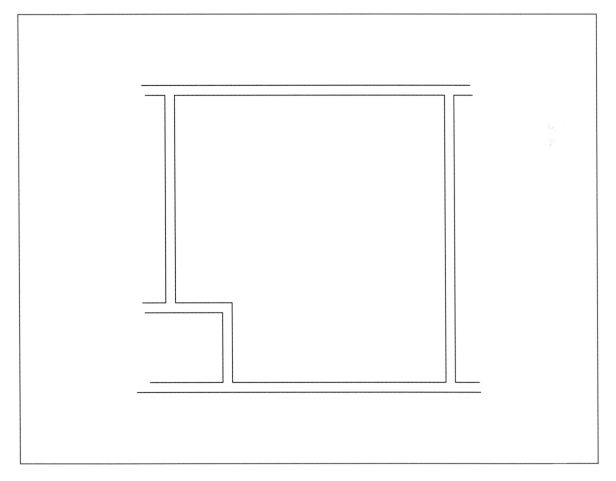

**Figure 4.2** Lightly pencil in the walls. (Concept by Mary Galloway, CKD–Alexandria, Virginia)

Tips:

- Avoid smearing the pencil lead. Lift your tools as you move them across the paper.

- Erase carefully so that you don't tear the paper.

- Use your drafting brush, not your hand, to remove eraser shavings and graphite.

**Step 4:** Locate the doors and windows. To ensure accuracy each opening should be located from at least two different reference points. Make sure that you show the door and window casing so that the overall dimensions listed for these openings are clearly different from the actual pass-through opening.

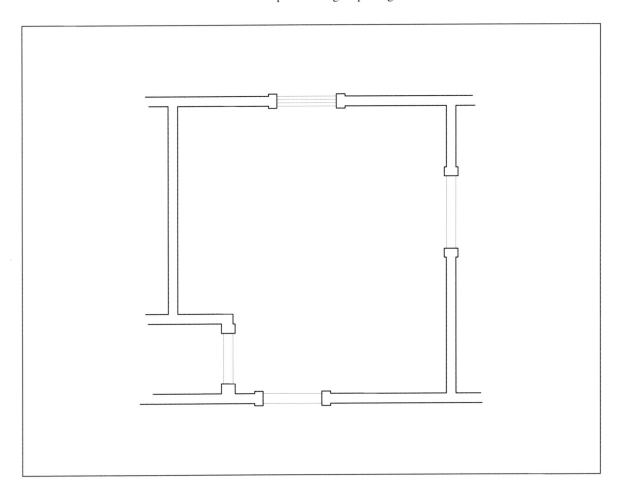

**Figure 4.3** Locate the doors and windows. (Concept by Mary Galloway, CKD–Alexandria, Virginia)

**Step 5:** Mistakes should be apparent but easily altered now because all your lines so far have been light layout lines. When all the measurements have been double checked, you can darken the final wall, window and door lines.

**Step 6:** The remaining major interior elements are next. These include cabinets, equipment, fixtures, furniture and clearances around these items. The interior elements are drawn in lightly at first and then darkened when everything is confirmed in final locations.

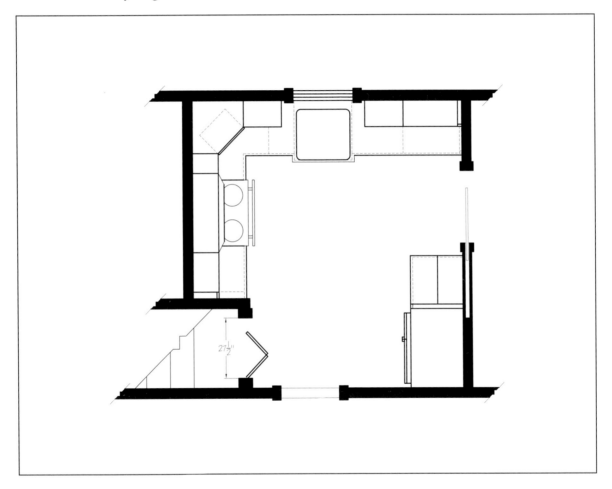

After the design has been finalized, darken all the solid object lines, such as tall and wall cabinets and countertops. Then draw the final base cabinet lines with hidden lines (short dashes). Use a straightedge with divided markings, such as those found on a template, to keep the dashes consistent.

**Figure 4.4** Add the major pieces of the design: cabinets, equipment fixtures and furniture. (Concept by Mary Galloway, CKD–Alexandria, Virginia)

**Step 7:** Draw in the dimension lines following a systematic method. Draw the line closest to the wall first, then the second and third set of lines. Locate the individual openings and sections of walls. Next, locate the centerlines of all appliances and plumbing fixtures, with long, short and long lines. Lastly, locate the total (overall) dimension for each wall. Do not forget to include the ceiling height in the center of the drawing, although you may leave this for Step 8.

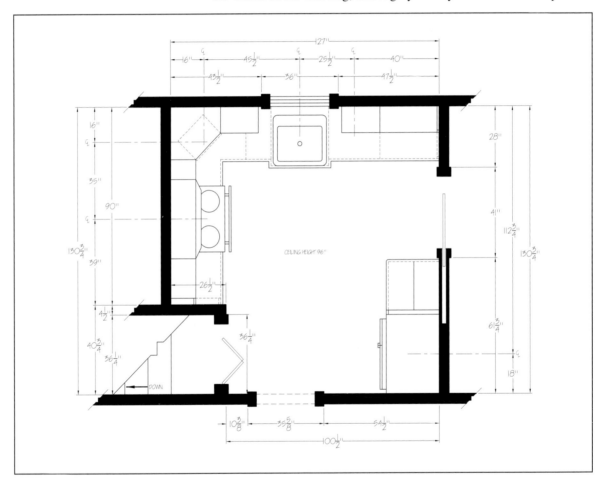

**Figure 4.5** Draw in the dimension lines. (Concept by Mary Galloway, CKD–Alexandria, Virginia)

**Step 8:** Now you are ready to put in the details. Add any nomenclature, notes and accessories, such as chairs and flooring.

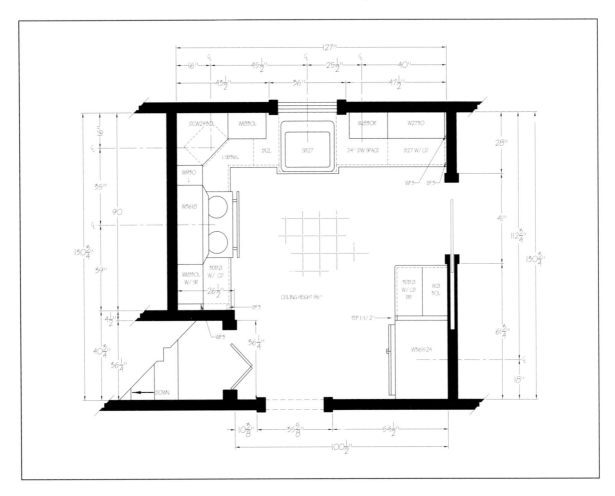

**Figure 4.6** Interior details and notes are added to complete the floor plan. (Concept by Mary Galloway, CKD–Alexandria, Virginia)

**Step 9:** Complete the list of specification details by matching them with corresponding numbers in the plan. Refer to the Graphic and Presentation Standards in Chapter 7 for further information.

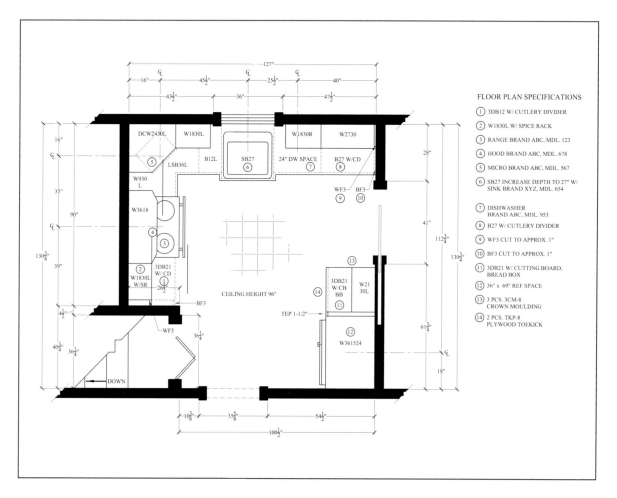

**Figure 4.7** Add the specifications. (Concept by Mary Galloway, CKD–Alexandria, Virginia)

See Chapter 8, page 142 for a larger, completed plan.

**Step 10:** Complete the title block. Identify your company, client information, job identification, drawing number, your name as the designer as well as the draftsperson's name, the date and scale. The title block may include additional information if desired.

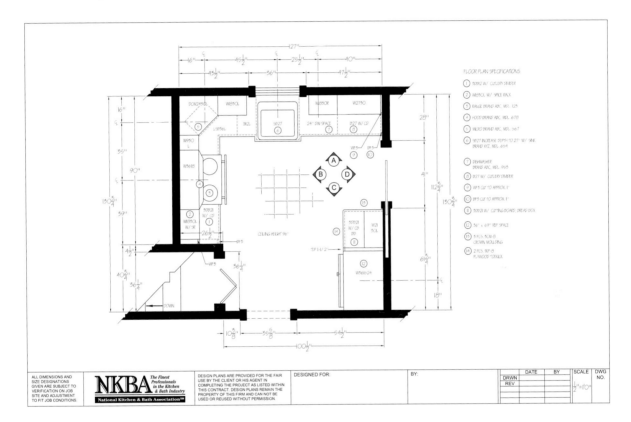

**Figure 4.8** Title block. (Concept by Mary Galloway, CKD–Alexandria, Virginia)

See Chapter 8, page 142 for a landscape example of the drawing and Appendix, page A1 for a fold-out example.

## DRAWING A
## MECHANICAL PLAN

Kitchen and bathroom project documents must include a mechanical plan because it communicates to the allied trades the exact location and specifications of all plumbing, electrical, heating, ventilation fixtures and equipment, and how they relate with the cabinetry.

The dimensions and cabinet layout are repeated but not the nomenclature or specifications. Rather, the mechanical plan shows the appropriate symbols as discussed in Chapter 3 with their descriptions listed in a legend. For example, all electrical appliances that require 120 volt electrical service will show a special purpose outlet symbol with initials corresponding to the appliance such as "DW" for dishwasher. Appliances requiring 240-volt service that are plugged in and not hard-wired use the circle with three parallel lines through it, for example as with an electric range.

**Figure 4.9** Mechanical plans indicate plumbing, electrical, heating and ventilation. (Concept by Mary Galloway, CKD–Alexandria, Virginia)

See Chapter 8, page 144 for a landscape example of the drawing and Appendix, page A3 for a fold-out example.

Ceiling fixtures such as lights, fans and vents are shown on a reflected ceiling plan. Reflected means that the ceiling fixtures are shown as if reflected onto the paper using a mirror. All ceiling-mounted fixtures must be dimensioned with centerlines within the walls of the mechanical plan as well as the heights of switches, outlets and receptacles.

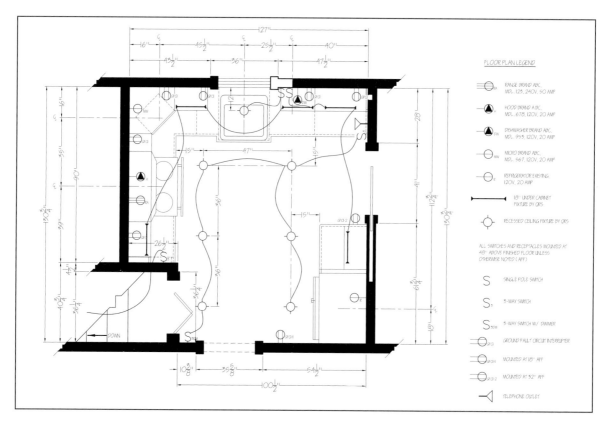

## DRAWING A
## CONSTRUCTION PLAN

A construction plan may be required if walls or openings will be altered from their original locations or other structural changes or additions are planned. A construction plan shows both the existing conditions of the structure or the architect's blueprint and the changes required to the building in order to accomplish your design. Note that any changes to the structure in any way must be approved by the builder, architect or licensed remodeler before proceeding with the project.

Special symbols clearly illustrate the construction alterations necessary. For example, a wall is shown solid or hollow if it is to remain unchanged; new walls to be constructed are shown with the appropriate material symbol; and existing openings to be closed are hatched with parallel lines. Universally accepted wall and partition symbols are indicated in Chapter 3. However, whether you use these or other symbols, your construction plan should always include a legend listing the symbol and its description.

**Figure 4.10** Construction plans illustrate existing and new construction. (Concept by Mary Galloway, CKD–Alexandria, Virginia)

See Chapter 8, page 143 for a landscape example of the drawing and Appendix, page A2 for a fold-out example.

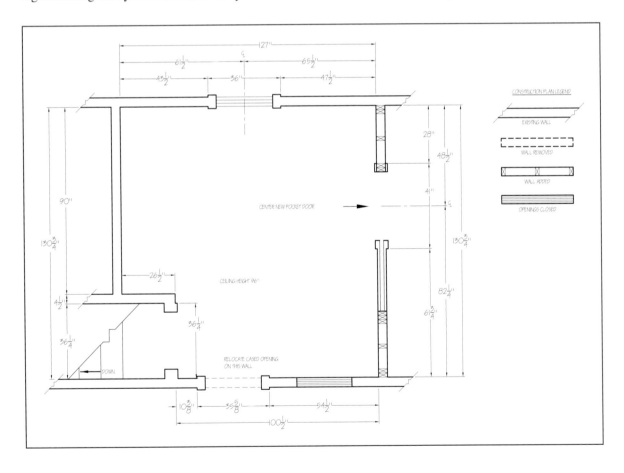

The construction plan should include only the walls, their dimensions and the legend. The dimensions should show the measurements of the interior finished surfaces. New windows and doors should be located from outside of the casing on each side of the window or door (sometimes called trim to trim). Additionally, new windows and doors should be noted by the manufacturer brand and model numbers whenever possible.

## DRAWING A COUNTERTOP PLAN

A separate countertop plan is not required with your presentation to the client since the outline is indicated on the floor plan. However, you may find a countertop plan helpful to illustrate the installation or fabrication to the allied tradesperson, particularly in complex projects, such as those that combine various counter materials or built-up edge treatments.

If you decide to include a countertop plan, show only the walls of the space and the outline of the cabinets, fixtures and equipment, applicable notes, details and dimensions. There may be up to three dimension lines for each counter section. The first dimension line shows the center of any cut-outs such as those for sinks and cooktops. Use the second dimension line to indicate the overall counter length. The final dimension indicates the overall available wall length.

Include notes about cut-outs, corner treatments, depth changes and such with arrows pointing to the specific area. A detailed profile of the counter edge treatment is often provided using a larger scale to clearly illustrate the counter design and its overhang relative to the face of the cabinet.

While the standard depth of a kitchen counter is 25 inches and a bathroom vanity is 22 inches, other factors may alter the depth such as inset, lipped or full overlay doors, and should therefore be noted. But typically a countertop overhangs the face of the door by $3/4$ to 1 inch. Therefore, it is critical to know the exact depth of the cabinet including the door. This level of detail helps to eliminate error by clearly communicating your ideas.

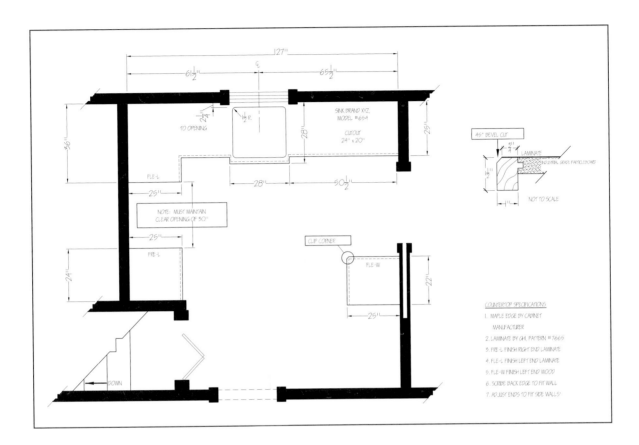

**Figure 4.11** Countertop plans help to convey details, such as custom edge treatments. (Concept by Mary Galloway, CKD–Alexandria, Virginia)

See Chapter 8, page 145 for a landscape example of the drawing.

## DRAWING A
## SOFFIT PLAN

A separate soffit plan is also not a required drawing for the client, but again, it may be helpful in conveying your design. Follow the same guidelines as provided for a countertop plan. If the soffit is complex, such as one with multiple levels or is stepped, exclude the cabinets to eliminate confusion. Be careful, though, to compare the soffit and cabinet dimensions in order to ensure consistent reveals. If the cabinets are included, always show the thickness of their doors or a notation of inset doors if they are used. Use the overhead line type to draw the soffit outline which is a line of long dashes. An elevation drawing of the soffit should be included on the soffit plan to further detail complex designs.

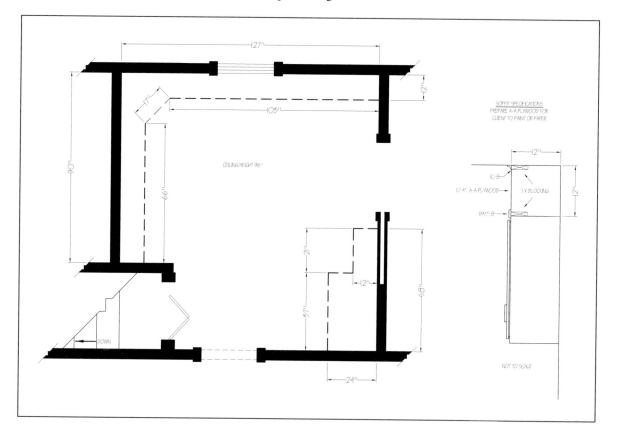

**Figure 4.12** Soffit plans use the overhead type of line. (Concept by Mary Galloway, CKD–Alexandria, Virginia)

See Chapter 8, page 146 for a landscape example of the drawing.

## INTERPRETIVE DRAWINGS

Elevations, paraline drawings and perspectives illustrate the vertical elements in a design not seen in a floor plan or any other overhead view of the design.

An elevation is an orthographic drawing just like the floor plan, but drawn from another viewpoint. Orthographic drawings are ones in which the lines of sight from points on the object to the picture plane of the image are perpendicular to that plane, and include floor plans, elevations, building sections, and site plans. An elevation drawing is a scaled drawing in both height and width, but not depth. Several views are usually required to properly illustrate the space. The various views should correspond with symbols on the floor plan indicating the views the elevation shows.

**Figure 4.13A** The elevations correspond directly to the plans. (Concept by Mary Galloway, CKD–Alexandria, Virginia)

See Chapter 8, page 147 for a landscape example of the drawing.

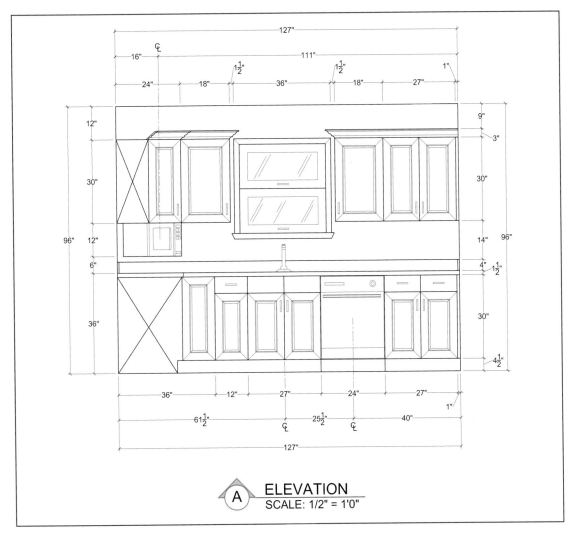

ELEVATION
SCALE: 1/2" = 1'0"

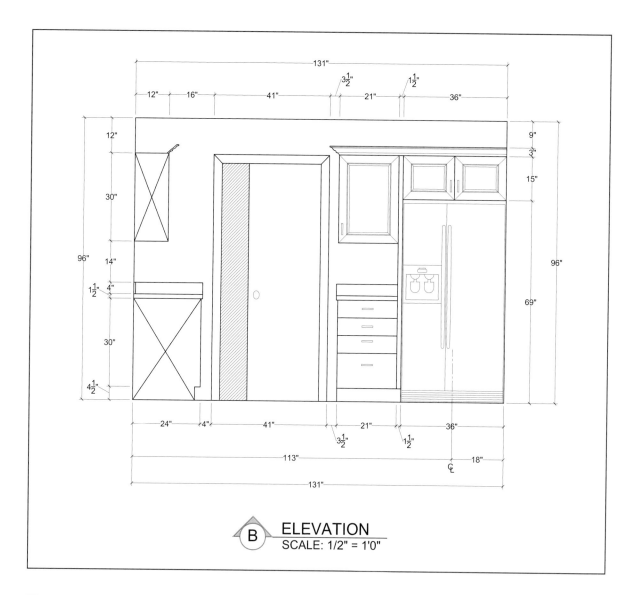

ELEVATION
SCALE: 1/2" = 1'0"

**Figure 4.13B** (Concept by Mary Galloway, CKD–Alexandria, Virginia)

See Chapter 8, page 148 for a landscape example of the drawing.

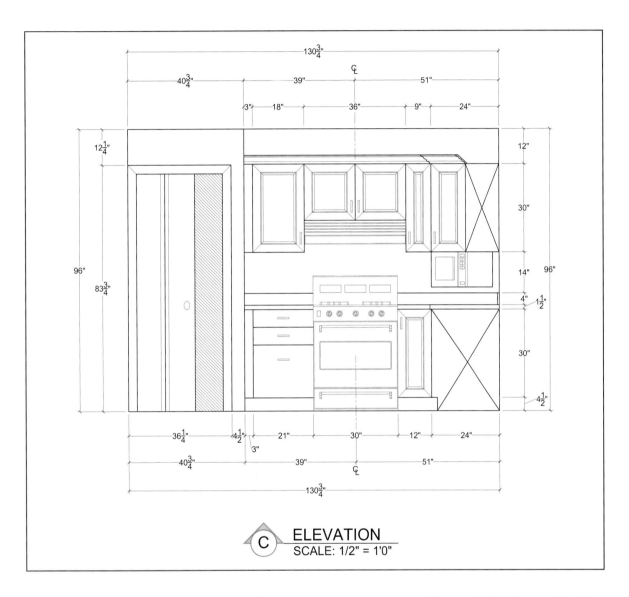

ELEVATION
SCALE: 1/2" = 1'0"

**Figure 4.13C** (Concept by Mary Galloway, CKD–Alexandria, Virginia)

See Chapter 8, page 149 for a landscape example of the drawing.

## PARALINE DRAWINGS

Paraline drawings, also referred to as "pictorial drawings," are similar to orthographic drawings, however, paraline drawings show an object as viewed from a skew direction in order to reveal all three directions. As mentioned earlier, elevations illustrate only width and height. A paraline drawing offers a view of three sides. Paraline drawings are used by designers to illustrate details when more than one side of an object needs to be shown. Often, the paraline drawing is sketched to illustrate the designer's ideas. But, if necessary, a paraline drawing can be scaled in all three directions. Unfortunately, three of the drawings below, when scaled, appear to be distorted. The 30° isometric, however, can be scaled and appears more pleasing to the eye. Many designers, when ordering modifications to cabinets, use the 30° isometric. It can be quickly drawn with a 30°/60° triangle.

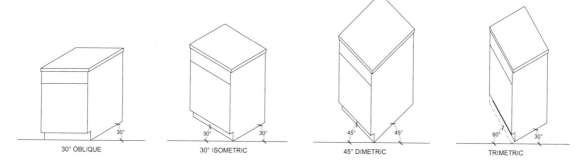

30° OBLIQUE     30° ISOMETRIC     45° DIMETRIC     TRIMETRIC

**Figure 4.14** Paraline drawings can help the design process.

## PERSPECTIVE DRAWINGS

A perspective drawing is a type of paraline drawing. Following are several examples which demonstrate hand-drawn and computer-generated perspectives. As you view these drawings, notice how each one takes on an individual personality. In time, you too will develop your own personal style depending on your needs and preferences. There are three qualities inherent to perspectives that separate them from other drawing types: a diminishing size in relation to distance; a vanishing or meeting of parallel lines as they recede; and a foreshortening of horizontal planes as they near the horizon line.

**Figure 4.15** Perspectives can also be used to help the designer visualize how the surfaces selected will relate to one another. (Courtesy of Sharon Armstrong, CKD, CBD–St. Petersburg, Florida)

There are three types of perspective drawings: two-point, one-point and bird's eye perspectives. The two-point view, which illustrates two walls, is usually preferred because it is the most realistic. Using two two-point perspective, drawings will completely represent a space since all or almost all of the walls will be depicted. A one-point perspective shows three walls where the center wall will basically be an elevation. Details are obscured and side walls can look crowded.

**Figure 4.16** One-point perspective drawing. (Courtesy of Peter Ross Salerno, CMKBD–Wyckoff, New Jersey)

**Figure 4.17** A one-point perspective computer generated image. (Courtesy of 20-20 Technologies, Inc.)

**Figure 4.18** A two-point perspective created using the construction method. (Courtesy of Barbara Herr–Marietta, Pennsylvania)

**Figure 4.19** A perspective created using computer software. (Courtesy of Planit)

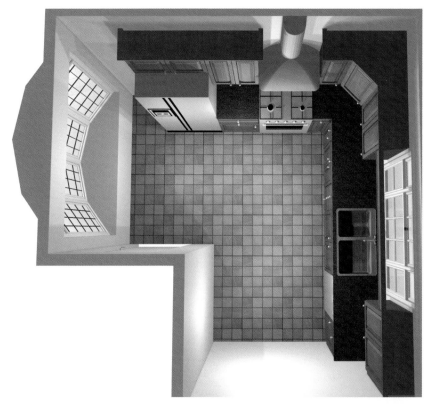

**Figure 4.20** Bird's eye perspective. (Courtesy of Planit)

A bird's eye perspective is recommended to illustrate small spaces. All the walls are seen because the view is from above looking down onto the floor. Think of it as looking down into a scale model. A bird's eye perspective is not realistic, but it does show the spatial relationship between the various pieces in the room.

In any type of perspective, the drawing process includes a station point. This is the point at which you are looking into the space; it is your station and is typically positioned at eye level. There are three ways to create a perspective: the construction method, the grid method, and using a computer. In the construction method, numerous points are plotted into position by drawing lines from every corner to a picture plane and then transferring these points to another location by connecting them with the vanishing point. The grid method is based on the construction method, but the transferring of points has been done. Grids are available at drafting supply stores and through Internet sites. Some computer-aided drawing software programs allow you to choose your station point and, with a click of the mouse, a perspective is generated.

## Enhancing the Drawing

The lines of a perspective define its limits, but the drawing is given realism by the addition of shading, highlights, color, people and accessories. With practice, your drawings will come to life. Add shading to floor plans and elevations to add interest. Be careful not to distract the viewer from important information.

Shading conveys even more information by defining dimension and direction. An otherwise flat object becomes three-dimensional by adding shadows. Shading can be done mechanically or freehand using lines, dots and tones. Because there are several light sources in an interior, it is difficult to calculate exact shadow delineation. Therefore, the standard practice is to consider two light sources: from the upper left and upper right. As you draw, think of the light shining over each shoulder and onto your drawing. The top and front surfaces of objects are in the most light and receive little or no shading. The sides of objects not in direct view, such as cabinet sides and the ceiling, are in a light shade. The darkest shades are reserved for areas below overhangs. The principles behind these types of shadows are:

- parallel surfaces create parallel shadow edges

- perpendicular surfaces create sloping shadow edges

Enhance depth perception by varying tonal values of shades. Two objects that appear equal in tone appear to be in the same spatial plane. Varying the shading tones of each object emphasizes its depth.

There are several principles that may be applied to produce this effect. In black line artwork, shading can show depth, texture and material. Color can help your client understand the design and show the texture of surfaces as in Figure 4.23. Blue rather than black or gray can be used to shade areas that will be naturally dark when the design is installed. When shading with pencil, the background can be blended by smudging the graphite and lightening it at the same time. These shading techniques can be done with pencil, pen or marker. Each medium has its own special look. The final presentation will vary depending on your choice of medium and personal style. By thickening edges, a drawing becomes easier to interpret and more real.

A

**Figure 4.21** Light sources casting shadows. (a. Courtesy of 20-20 Technologies, Inc. b. Courtesy of Planit.)

B

**Figure 4.22** Shading a drawing using gray tones. (Courtesy of Tony Hunt, CKD, CBD–Toronto, Ontario)

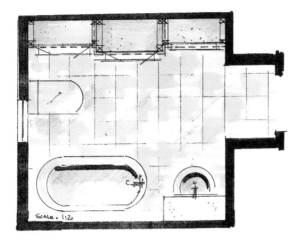

**Figure 4.23** Shading a drawing using color. (Courtesy of Ines Hanl–Victoria, British Columbia)

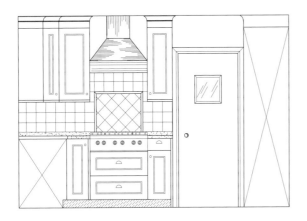

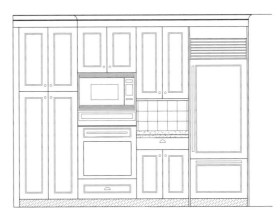

**Figure 4.24** Shading a drawing using pencil. (Courtesy of Nancy Stern–Riverdale, New Jersey)

People and accessories also add realism to drawings. There are several books available with line art that can be traced by placing the art under the drawing. Other good sources are your local newspaper advertisement section and department store catalogues. If the size is not exactly right, reduce or enlarge it on a copy machine and then trace it into your drawing. Remember that when you add people and accessories, they will typically block a piece of your drawing, like the cabinets or an appliance. Position these extras carefully so as not to distract from your design. Never block something that you especially want to show. Scanned art can be added to your computer-generated drawings and saved making it available when you need it again. You may even want to consider using digital photographs of your clients, their own accessories and personal items and the views they will see from their new windows. These will make your design real to your clients.

**Figure 4.25** Accessories add a realistic touch. (Courtesy of St. Charles of New York)

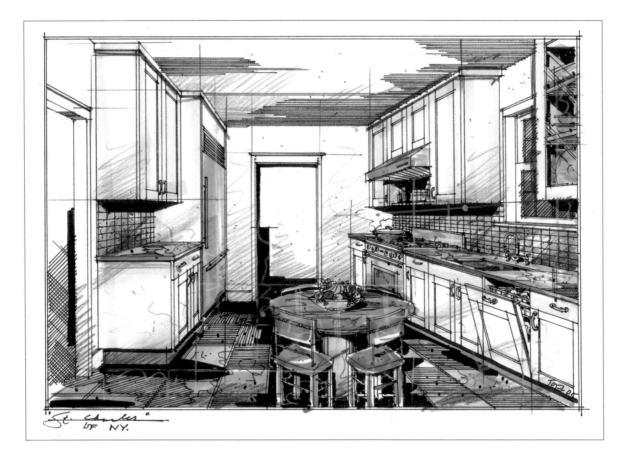

**Figure 4.26** Examples of color perspectives. (Courtesy of Kathie Maughan–Portland, Oregon)

Color is the ultimate enhancement. It evokes emotion and has a far reaching effect on the viewer's perception of the design. When selecting a coloring medium, be sure to also purchase black and several shades of cool gray. Begin your color collection with subtle, muted tones and neutral tones rather than the bright primary colors. They may look nice, but as with people and accessories enhancements, they can overwhelm the drawing. You will also want to be sure that the colors you choose will be a close match to the actual colors that will be used. Color on a perspective can be very helpful but can be a disappointment if the finished space is not what the client saw on your drawing. Less is more when applying color: hint at it in different areas; use markers and pencils together to complement each other. Using colored pencils alone will add texture and highlights; or go over the marker base with them to soften the effect.

# Chapter 5: Designing Kitchens and Baths Using Computers

There is one tool that has permanently changed the way kitchen and bathroom design companies do business and it is the computer. Like every other aspect of our lives, the computer has made kitchen and bathroom design and business management easier, faster, and more convenient for both the designer and the consumer. The program's automated features allow you to try a number of options on the screen without having to spend a lot of time locating manufacturer's specifications books. Also available are software programs for accounting, inventory and management of clients' projects. There are many software programs developed specifically for the kitchen and bathroom industry. A search of "kitchen and bathroom design software" on the Internet will give you a lot of choices when you begin researching which program will work best for you.

## SOFTWARE PROGRAMS

Because of their speed and accuracy, computers are a powerful asset. With a few clicks of a mouse, a kitchen or bathroom can practically appear before your eyes. There are programs where you type in the dimensions of the room, select windows, doors and equipment and their placement, and the computer completes the design, placing cabinets, fillers, tile and other products. A complete set of working drawings can be created in minutes.

You will think of many different configurations and materials choices during the first phase of the design process. Most of the software programs available allow you to change your mind as often as new ideas come to you, automatically adjusting the prices each time you rework the design. Manufacturer's catalogs have been incorporated into many design software programs so you have numerous options from which to choose.

Some other handy features may include three-dimensional views, realistic, photo-quality images and virtual tours of your design. These are the things that will give you and the client a true sense of what the new space will look like. However, these features should be used with caution: the finished design will indeed be different than the computer-generated images. You want the client to understand that there will be variations between the actual products and the pictures printed from the computer.

A

**Figure 5.1** Examples of computer-generated drawings. (a. Courtesy of Planit. b. Courtesy of 20-20 Technologies, Inc.)

B

## Computer-Aided Drafting

There are also traditional drafting software programs that act as a drafting tool and are known as computer-aided drafting (CAD) software programs. Using various commands, you draw the design on the computer screen with a mouse, digitizer or stylus, instead of on paper. A CAD program can be individually customized by the user and is limited only by the designer's imagination. These programs are broad in scope and are not limited to just kitchens and bathrooms; complete homes and other building structures can be created.

**Figure 5.2** Example of a realistic image. (Courtesy of 20-20 Technologies, Inc.)

With technology comes technical problems and questions. Design software companies have training and technical support available. As you shop for a software program, look at the training offerings. Many have onsite training where they come to your business to teach your staff the features of the software. You can attend courses at sites the software company determines or at their location. At the very least, a technical support staff is available when on-the-spot questions arise. The ease of getting help is something that should be as important as the design features of the program.

**Figure 5.3** Example of a realistic image. (Courtesy of Planit)

NKBA encourages the use of any tool that will assist you in your kitchen and bath design business. Make sure you do your homework to find the best program for you. Be advised, however, that these computer drafting programs may not be able to create drawings according to NKBA's Graphics and Presentation Standards discussed in this book. Also, NKBA does not endorse any computer program.

# Chapter 6: Presenting the Project

At some point, you will present your projects to a client, a potential employer, attendees at a home show, or someone else. Therefore, you need to decide which presentation style suits you, depending on where you will be presenting and the best way to show off the project. This chapter focuses on presenting hard copies of project documents. NKBA's *Kitchen & Bath Business Management* provides ideas for electronically presenting your portfolio, including CDs, DVDs, etc., as well as on your website.

## DRAWING PORTFOLIO

One way to present a project is to create a portfolio that allows you to put the drawings into acetate or plastic sleeves and flip through them like a book. A portfolio no larger than 18" x 24" is easy to carry and small enough to show the client at a table or desk in your office. Some smaller portfolios stand to resemble a tabletop easel for convenient viewing. You may also consider a notebook-style presentation that can be given to the client once the project is installed. Contact information for your company and the manufacturers' products selected can be inserted so the client has one source to go to when questions arise after the project is complete.

You may prefer to show the project mounted on matte board or foam core board and displayed on an easel. Each drawing is mounted onto individual boards using a spray adhesive on the back of the drawing. The board is usually cut to the same size as the drawing. Some designers add a matte around it as a frame or cut off the title block, leaving just the drawing and adding a colored border with marker or tape. If time allows or the presentation warrants it, add materials samples, appliance photographs and other items to complete the presentation, referred to as a sample or concept board.

## Notebook Presentations

Consider what you will do with your project drawings after completing each job. Perhaps make an album of before and after photographs, placing them next to reduced drawings of the new designs. This becomes a great portfolio to show prospective clients who visit your showroom and is easily transported to home shows. Keep in mind that you should be collecting your projects in a portfolio for future job interviews.

**Figure 6.1** Small, medium and table-top portfolios protect your project while making it easy to present. (Courtesy of Alvin & Co., Inc.)

**Figure 6.2** Notebook presentations are compact and convenient. (Courtesy of Alvin & Co., Inc.)

**Figure 6.3** Mounted and/or matted projects are a standard way to present projects. (Courtesy of NKBA)

### Storage

After you have completed the drawings, you will need a way to safely store them. The type of presentation you choose may be the best way to store the project. For example, a shelf of notebooks, one for each client, can be very handy. Some companies prefer to store all their projects in a cabinet with shallow drawers designed to accommodate large drawings. Cabinets made of cardboard may have drawers that pull out individually to be easily taken to a presentation. Many designers still prefer to roll large drawings and store them in tubes. This can be convenient if you need to mail drawings, but rolled drawings make presentations more difficult because the drawings do not lay flat and need to be weighted on the ends while you show each one.

**Figure 6.4** Examples of storage for drawings. (Courtesy of NKBA)

# Chapter 7: NKBA's Graphics and Presentation Standards

NKBA's *Graphics and Presentation Standards for Kitchen and Bathroom Design* are included in this book so that you might gain a better and clearer insight into the concepts for good presentation techniques. Their use is strongly recommended because they contain a specific set of criteria which, when applied by the kitchen and bathroom specialist, produce professional project documents that include the following:

- floor plan

- construction plan

- mechanical plan

- interpretive drawings (elevations, perspective drawings, oblique, dimetric, isometric and trimetric drawings and sketches)

- specifications

- design statement

Two sample sets of project documents are included in the next chapter, one of a kitchen and one of a bathroom.

## PURPOSE

By standardizing floor plans and presentation drawings, kitchen and bathroom designers will:

- limit errors caused by misinterpreting the floor plan.

- avoid misreading dimensions, which can result in costly errors.

- prevent cluttering floor plans and drawings with secondary information, which often makes the documents difficult to interpret.

- create a clear understanding of the scope of the project for everyone involved in the job.

- present a professional image to the client.

- permit faster processing of orders.

- simplify estimating and specification preparation.

- help in the standardization of uniform nomenclature and symbols.

## THE KITCHEN OR BATH FLOOR PLAN

The floor plan should depict the entire room when possible. When the entire room cannot be depicted, it must show the area where cabinetry and appliances are permanently installed and must be divided by "break lines" (‾‾‾‾⟋) and must show all major structural elements with adjoining areas indicated and labeled. The floor plan must show all major structural elements such as walls, door swings, door openings, partitions, windows, archways and equipment.

- Kitchen and bath floor plans should be drawn to a scale of $1/2$ inch equals 1 foot ($1/2" = 1'-0"$) or the metric equivalent, (1cm = 20cm).

- Base cabinetry should be depicted using a dashed line (------); wall and tall cabinets, countertops, flooring material, furniture, appliances and fixtures not hidden by another object are depicted using a solid line.

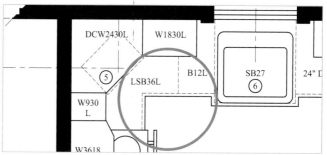

- A separate plan for the soffit is required when it is a different depth than the wall or tall cabinet below it. A separate soffit plan is also recommended when the soffit is to be installed prior to the wall or tall cabinet installation.

## TIPS FROM THE PROS

The acceptable paper for the original drawings of the floor plan, construction plan, mechanical plan and interpretive drawings is set at a minimum of 11 inches x 17 inches. Translucent vellum tracing paper, imprinted with a black border and appropriate space available for the insertion of pertinent information, is strongly recommended. Copies of original drawings should appear in blue or black ink only on white paper. Ozalid or photocopy prints are acceptable. The use of lined yellow note paper, typing paper, scored graph paper or scored quadrille paper is not acceptable.

## Dimensions:

- All drawing dimensions used on kitchen and bathroom floor plans must be given in inches and fractions of inches only, (i.e. 124 $^1/4$"). Combining dimensions listed in feet and inches or the exclusive use of dimensions listed in feet and inches, 10' 4 $^1/4$" is not acceptable and should not be used under any circumstances. Again, this would also apply to the metric equivalent.

- Each set of dimensions should be at least $^3/16$ inches apart on separate dimension lines which are to intersect with witness lines. These intersecting points should be indicated by arrows, dots or slashes. (See page 48 for a description of dimension lines.)

- All dimensions should be shown outside the wall lines whenever possible

- All dimensions should be listed parallel to the title block at the bottom of the vellum paper and break the dimension line near its mid-point. This mechanical drafting technique eliminates errors in reading dimensions.

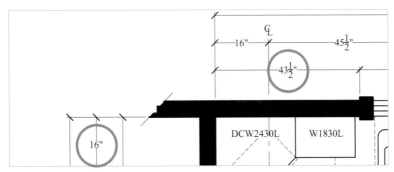

- An acceptable alternative is to draw all dimensions and lettering so that it is readable from the bottom edge or the right side of the plans.

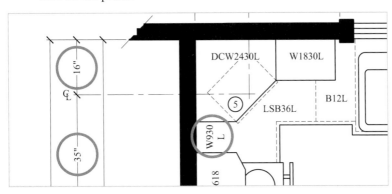

• Finished interior dimensions are used on all project documents to denote available space for cabinetry and/or other types of equipment. If the kitchen/bathroom specialist is responsible for specifying the exact method of wall construction, finish and/or partition placement, the specialist should include partition centerlines on the construction plan, as well as the finished interior dimensions.

The following dimensions must be shown on every floor plan as minimum requirements.

• Overall length of wall areas to receive cabinets, countertops, fixtures, or any equipment occupying floor and/or wall space. This dimension should always be the outside line.

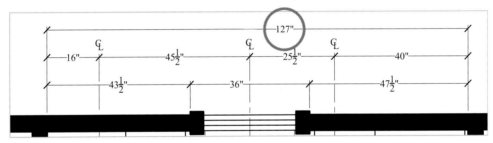

• Each wall opening (windows, arches, and doors), major appliances and fixed structures (chimneys, protrusions and partitions) must be individually dimensioned. Dimensions are shown from outside trim. Trim size must be noted in the specification list. Fixtures such as radiators remaining in place must be outlined on the floor plan. These critical dimensions should be the first dimension line.

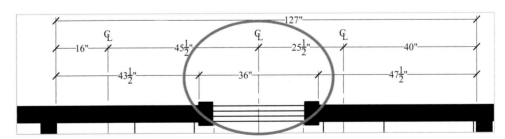

- Ceiling heights should appear on the floor plan.

- Additional notes must be included for any deviation from standard height, width and depth (cabinets, countertops, etc.).

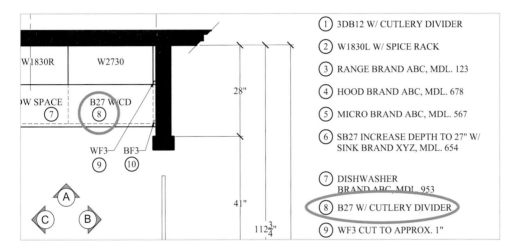

- The exact opening must be given in height, width and depth for areas to be left open to receive equipment, cabinets, appliances and fixtures at a future date.

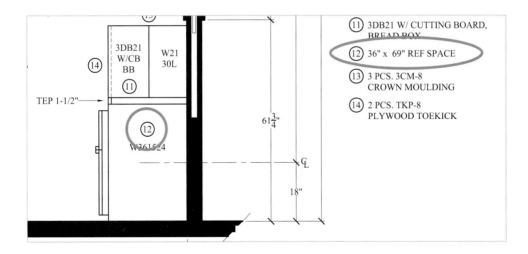

- Items such as island and peninsula cabinets must be shown with the overall dimensions given from countertop edge to the opposite countertop edge, tall cabinet or wall. The exact location of the structure must be identified by dimensions which position it from two directions: from return walls or from the face of cabinets/equipment opposite the structure.

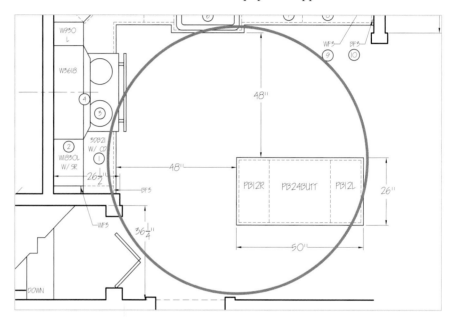

**Centerline Dimensions:**

- Centerline dimensions must be given for equipment in two directions when possible to indicate the exact location of the equipment for plumbing and wiring purposes.

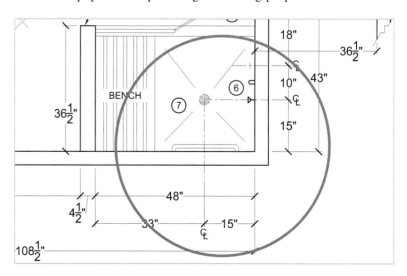

- Items requiring centerline include: all appliances, sinks, tubs/showers, toilets, bidets, fan units, light fixtures, heating and air conditioning ducts, and radiators.

- Centerline dimensions should be pulled from return walls or from the front of cabinets/equipment opposite the mechanical element.

- Centerlines on the mechanical plan will be indicated by the symbol ( ℄ ) followed by a long-short-long broken line that extends into the floor area.

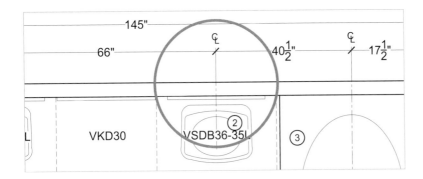

- When the centerline dimension line is outside the floor area, it is typically shown as the second (and, if required, the third) line following the dimension line which identifies the individual wall segments.

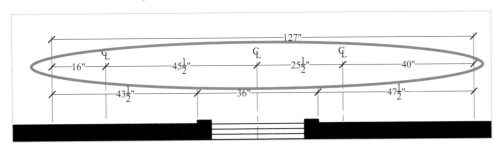

**Cabinets, Appliances and Equipment Nomenclature and Designation:**

- Cabinets should be designated and identified by manufacturer nomenclature inside the area to indicate their position.

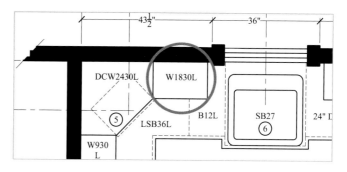

- Cabinet system trim and finish items are designated outside their area, with an arrow clarifying exactly where the trim piece is located.

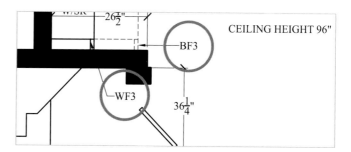

- To ensure clarity, some design firms prefer to number and call out all the cabinet nomenclature in the floor plan specification listing. Equally acceptable is the use of a circle reference number to designate each cabinet on the floor plan, and elevations with the cabinet code listed within the individual unit width on the elevations or in a separate cross-reference list on the elevations.

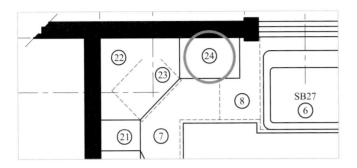

- Regardless of the cabinet designation system selected, additional information for supplementary fixtures, appliances, equipment, accessories and special provisions pertaining to the cabinets must be indicated within the cabinet or equipment area by a reference number in a circle. This additional information should then be listed in the specifications on the floor plan drawing or a separate sheet of paper.

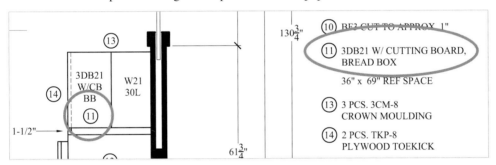

- Special order materials or custom design features, angled cabinets, unusual tops, molding, trim details, etc. should be shown in a section view, (sometimes referred to as a "cut view"), a plan view in a scale larger than ( $1/2" = 1'-0"$) or in elevation view. Refer to Chapter 8 for sample plans.

For more information on cabinet nomenclature, see NKBA's *Kitchen & Bath Products.*

## THE CONSTRUCTION PLAN

The purpose of the construction plan is to show the relationship of the existing space with that of the new design. Because of the detail involved, construction information is detailed separately so that it does not clutter the floor plan. However, if construction changes are minimal, it is acceptable to combine the construction plan with either the floor plan or mechanical plan. (See pages 143 and 161 for sample construction plans.)

### Construction Plan Symbols

- Existing walls are shown as darkened spaces or hollow outlines.

- Wall sections to be removed are shown with an outline of broken lines.

- New walls show the material symbols applicable to the type of construction or use a symbol which is identified in the legend in order to distinguish them from existing partitions.

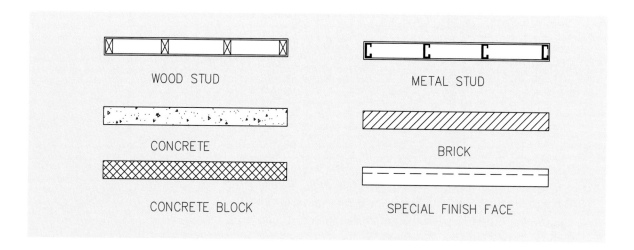

WOOD STUD

METAL STUD

CONCRETE

BRICK

CONCRETE BLOCK

SPECIAL FINISH FACE

**Figure 7.1** Construction plan symbols.

## THE MECHANICAL
## PLAN AND SYMBOLS

A separate plan for the mechanical systems will help to clearly identify such work without cluttering the floor plan. Refer to page 144 and 162 for sample plans.

- The mechanical plan should show an outline of the cabinets, countertops and fixtures without nomenclature.

- The mechanicals should be placed in the proper location with the proper symbols.

- All overall room dimensions should be listed.

- The mechanical plan will consist of the electrical/lighting, plumbing, heating, air conditioning and ventilation systems. If any minor wall or door construction changes are part of the plan, they should also be detailed on the mechanical plan, or on a separate plan.

- A mechanical legend should be prepared on the plan. This legend will be used to describe the symbols for special purpose outlets, fixtures or equipment.

- Centerline dimensions must be given for all equipment in two directions when possible.

- Items requiring centerline include: all appliances, sinks, tubs/showers, toilets, bidets, fan units, light fixtures, heating and air conditioning ducts, and radiators.

- Centerline dimensions should be pulled from return walls or from the face of item being centerlined to a position opposite it.

- Centerlines on the mechanical plan are to be indicated by the symbol followed by a long-short-long broken line that extends into the floor area.

**Figure 7.2** The centerline symbol.

## INTERPRETIVE DRAWINGS

Interpretive drawings are used as an explanatory means of understanding the floor plans. Under no circumstances should the interpretive drawings be used as a substitute for floor plans. In cases of dispute, the floor plans are the legally binding document. The following are considered interpretive drawings: elevations, perspectives, oblique, dimetric, isometric, trimetric drawings and sketches. (See Chapter 4 for more details.) Because perspective drawings are not dimensioned to scale, a disclaimer should be included on the drawing, such as:

THIS DRAWING IS AN ARTISTIC INTERPRETATION OF THE GENERAL APPEARANCE OF THE FLOOR PLAN. IT IS NOT MEANT TO BE AN EXACT RENDITION.

Elevations must show a full front view of all wall areas receiving cabinets and equipment as shown on the floor plan. A portion of the cabinet doors and drawer front should indicate style and, when applicable, placement of handles/pulls. All cabinets, appliances, countertops, fixtures and equipment in the elevation are dimensioned as follows:

- Cabinets with toekick and finished height (see example on page 147.)

- Cabinet widths

- Countertops; indicate countertop thickness and show back splash height

- All doors, windows and other openings in walls which will receive equipment. The window/door casing or trim will be listed within the overall opening dimensions.

- All permanent fixtures

- All main structural elements and protrusions such as chimneys, partitions, etc.

- Centerlines for all mechanical elements and plumbing

Perspectives are not drawn to scale. Grids can be used under vellum paper to accurately portray a perspective rendering. Designers have the option of preparing a one-point or two-point perspective with or without the use of a grid.

- Perspectives should be a reasonably correct representation of the longest cabinet or fixture run, or the most important area in terms of usage.

- Perspectives need not show the complete kitchen or bathroom.

- Separate sectional views of significant areas or features are considered acceptable.

Oblique, dimetric, isometric and trimetric are several types of interpretive drawings that can be used to illustrate special cabinets and features such as countertops or special order cabinets where mechanical representation and dimensions are important.

Sketches are a quick way to achieve a total picture of the kitchen or bathroom without exact details in scaled dimensions. A sketch can be studied, adjusted and sketched over, as the designer and client are discussing the most satisfactory layout for the space.

**Figure 7.3** A quick sketch can serve as a guide for drawing an exact plan of the space.

## SPECIFICATIONS

Depending on the complexity of the job, specifications may appear on the plan, or they may be listed on a separate form, or a combination of both. Either way, they are part of the project documents.

Examples of NKBA's Specification Forms, available to members, appear in Chapter 8.

The purpose of the project specifications is to clearly define the details of the products listed and the scope and limits of the job. They:

- define the area of responsibility between the kitchen/bathroom specialist and the purchaser.

- should clearly define all material and work affected by the job, either directly or indirectly.

- must clearly indicate which individual has the ultimate responsibility for all or part of the above.

- should contain descriptive references to all areas of work.

All specification categories must be completed. If the job does not cover any given area, "Not Applicable," "N/A," or "None" should be inserted. In each area, the responsibility of either the kitchen/bathroom specialist or the owner or the owner's agent must be assigned. In all cases, the owner and the owner's agent must receive a completed copy of the project documents prior to the commencement of any work.

Project Responsibilities

- Kitchen/bathroom designers are responsible for the accuracy of the dimensioned floor plans and the selections and designations of all cabinets, appliances and equipment, if made or approved by them.

- Any equipment directly purchased by the kitchen/bathroom specialist for resale should be the responsibility of the kitchen/bathroom designer. Further, the specialist must be responsible for supplying product installation instructions to the owner or the owner's agent.

- Any labor furnished by the kitchen/bathroom designer, whether by their own employees or through sub-contractors paid directly by them and working under their direction, should be the kitchen/bathroom designer's responsibility. There should not be a delegation of total responsibility to the sub-contractor working under these conditions.

- Any equipment purchased directly by the owner or the owner's agent from an outside source should be the responsibility of the owner or the owner's agent. The same applies to any sub-contractor, building contractor, or other labor directly hired and/or paid by the owner or the owner's agent.

## DESIGN STATEMENT

The purpose of the design statement is to interpret the design problem and solution in order to substantiate the project to the client. Design statements may be verbal or written. It is important that a design statement be clear, concise and interesting to the reader. Written statements may be in either paragraph or bulleted/outline format. A design statement should be between 250 and 500 words. It may be a separate document, part of the working drawings or a combination of both. Refer to page 151 and 171 for samples. Design statements should clearly outline:

- design considerations and challenges of the project including, but not limited to: construction budget requirements, client needs and wants, special requests and lifestyle factors.

- form, function, economy, time requirements are typical organization means of stating design problems.

- how the designer arrived at the solutions and addressed the design considerations and challenges for the project.

- aesthetic considerations such as use of the principles and elements of design (i.e. pattern preferences, finish, color, surface selections and other details).

## TITLING PROJECT DOCUMENTS

When you design a project for a client, you must protect yourself from liability when referring to the drawings and you must protect the drawings themselves from being copied by your competitors. The entire set of paperwork, which includes your design plans, specifications and contract, can be referred to as the Project Documents.

When presenting the drawings for a kitchen or bathroom, NKBA recommends that you refer to the drawings as Kitchen Design Plans or Bathroom Design Plans. The design plans should have the following statement included on them in an obvious location in large or block letters.

DESIGN PLANS ARE NOT PROVIDED FOR ARCHITECTURAL OR ENGINEERING USE. IT IS THE RESPECTIVE TRADES' RESPONSIBILITY TO VERIFY THAT ALL INFORMATION LISTED IS IN ACCORDANCE WITH EQUIPMENT USE, APPLICABLE CODES AND ACTUAL JOBSITE DIMENSIONS.

The individual drawings incorporated in the overall kitchen or bathroom design presentation must also be carefully labeled. It is suggested that you refer to these other drawings as Floor Plans, Elevations, Mechanical Plans and Artist Renderings. NKBA suggests that you include a notation on the Artist Rendering drawings which reads:

THIS RENDERING IS AN ARTIST'S INTERPRETATION OF THE GENERAL APPERANCE OF THE ROOM. IT IS NOT INTENDED TO BE A PRECISE DEPICTION.

Never refer to a design plan as an architectural drawing or even as an architectural-type drawing. Do not include the words "architecture," "architectural design," "architectural phase," "architectural background," or any other use of the word "architectural" in any project documents that you prepare, in any of your business stationary, promotional information or any presentation materials. Any such reference to the work that you do or documents that you prepare may result in a violation of various state laws. A court may determine that your use of the word "architecture" or "architectural" could reasonably lead a client to believe that you possess a level of expertise that you do not. Worse yet, a court may find you liable for fraud and/or misrepresentation.

Laws do vary per state; therefore, it is important that you consult with your own legal counsel to be sure that you are acting within the applicable statutes in your area. You must clearly understand what drawings you are legally allowed to prepare and what drawings must be prepared under the auspices of a licensed architect or engineer.

**COPYRIGHT AND OWNERSHIP**

After drafting the design plans for your client, you should ensure that they will not be copied or used by a competitor. This may be done by copyrighting the design plans you prepare. Copyrighting is an international form of protection/exclusivity provided by law to authors of original works, despite whether the work is published or not. Original works of authorship include any literary, pictorial, graphic or sculptured works, such as your design plans, provided they are original works done by you. Copyright protection exists from the moment the work is created in its final form and will endure 50 years after your death.

If two or more persons are authors of an original work, they will be deemed co-owners of its copyright. For example, if you collaborate with an interior designer, you will both be co-owners of the design copyright. An original work generated by two or more authors is referred to as a joint work. Generally, a joint work results if the authors collaborated on the work or if each prepared a segment of it with the knowledge and intent that it would be incorporated with the contributions submitted by other authors. Accordingly, a joint work will only be found when each co-author intended his respective contribution to be combined into a larger, integrated piece. There is no requirement that each of the co-authors work together or even be acquainted with one another.

A work created by an employee within the scope of his employment is regarded as "work made for hire" and is normally owned by the employer, unless the parties explicitly stipulate in a written agreement, signed by both, that the copyright will be owned by the employee. If you are an independent contractor, the "work made for hire" statute does not include drawings or other design plans. Therefore, the copyright in any kitchen or bath design created by you will remain vested with you until you contractually agree to relinquish ownership.

To secure copyright protection for your plans, you are required to give notice of copyright on all publicly distributed copies. The use of the copyright notice is your responsibility as the copyright owner and does not require advance permission from, or registration with, the Copyright Office in Washington, D.C.

A proper copyright notice must include the following three items:

1. The symbol © or the word "Copyright" or the abbreviation "Copy." (the © is accepted as the international symbol);

2. The year of the first publication of the work;

3. The name of the owner of the copyright in the work, or an abbreviation by which the name can be recognized or a generally known alternative designation of the owner.

The notice should be affixed to all copies of your design plans in such a manner and location as to give reasonable notice of the claim of copyright. An example of a proper copyright notice would be:

COPYRIGHT © 2006 JOE SMITH

As mentioned previously, you or your firm continue to retain copyright protection of your design plan even if the plan is given to the client after he has paid for it. Although the copyright ownership may be transferred, such transfer must be in writing and signed by you as the owner of the copyright conveyed. Normally, the transfer of a copyright is made by contract. In order to protect your exclusive rights, however, you should include a clause in your contract which reads:

DESIGN PLANS ARE PROVIDED FOR THE FAIR USE BY THE CLIENT OR HIS AGENT IN COMPLETING THE PROJECT AS LISTED WITHIN THIS CONTRACT. DESIGN PLANS REMAIN THE PROPERTY OF (YOUR NAME) AND CANNOT BE USED OR REUSED WITHOUT PERMISSION.

This clause should also be in any agreement between you and a client who requests that you prepare a design plan for his review. Such a design plan usually serves as the basis for a subsequent contract between you and the client for the actual installation of the kitchen or bathroom. This type of agreement will prevent the client from obtaining a design plan from you and then taking that plan to a competitor who may simply copy it. As long as you retain the copyright in the design plan, you will be able to sue for infringement any party who has copied your design.

# Chapter 8: Sample Kitchen & Bathroom Project Documents

Two sets of sample project documents have been prepared according to the NKBA Graphics and Presentation Standards, one for a kitchen and one for a bathroom. They include:

- Title page              below
- Floor plan              kitchen, page 142; bath, page 160
- Construction plan   kitchen, page 143; bath, page 161
- Mechanical plan    kitchen, page 144; bath, page 162
- Countertop plan    kitchen, page 145; bath, page 163
- Soffit plan              kitchen, page 146; bath, page 164
- Elevations             kitchen, page 147–149; bath, page 165–168
- Perspectives         kitchen, page 150; bath, page 169–170
- Design Statement  kitchen, page 151; bath, page 171
- Specifications       kitchen, page 152; bath, page 172

**Figure 8.1** An example of a title page.

PROPOSED KITCHEN DESIGN FOR:

## JOHN & JANE SMITH

DRAWINGS GUIDE:

| | |
|---|---|
| FLOOR PLAN & SPECIFICATIONS | DWG 1–2 |
| CONSTRUCTION PLAN | DWG 3 |
| MECHANICAL PLAN | DWG 4 |
| ELEVATIONS | DWG 5–10 |
| CEILING & SOFFIT PLAN /DETAILS | DWG 11–12 |
| COLOR RENDERINGS | DWG 13–16 |

# SAMPLE KITCHEN PLANS

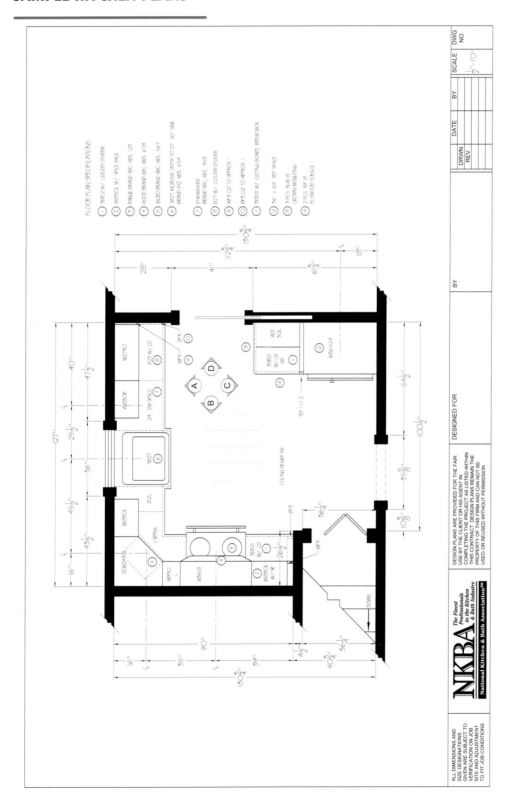

**Figure 8.2** Kitchen floor plan.

See Appendix, page A1 for a fold-out example.

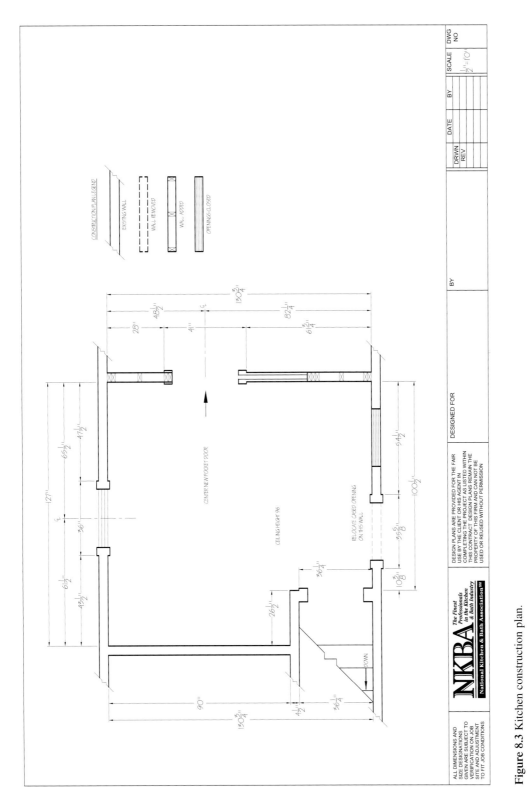

**Figure 8.3** Kitchen construction plan.

See Appendix, page A2 for a fold-out example.

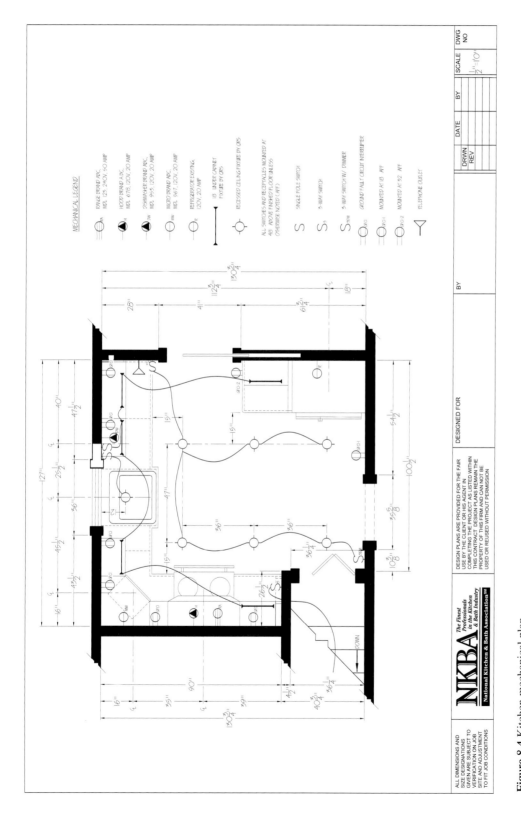

**Figure 8.4** Kitchen mechanical plan.

See Appendix, page A3 for a fold-out example.

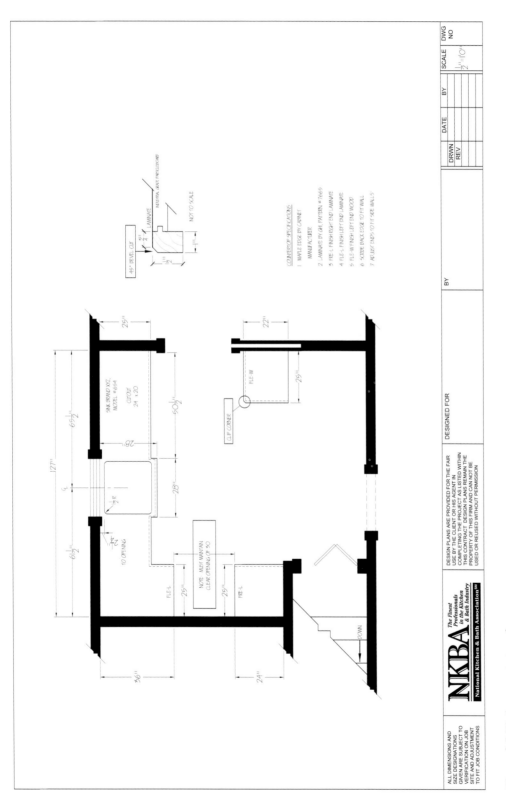

**Figure 8.5** Kitchen countertop plan.

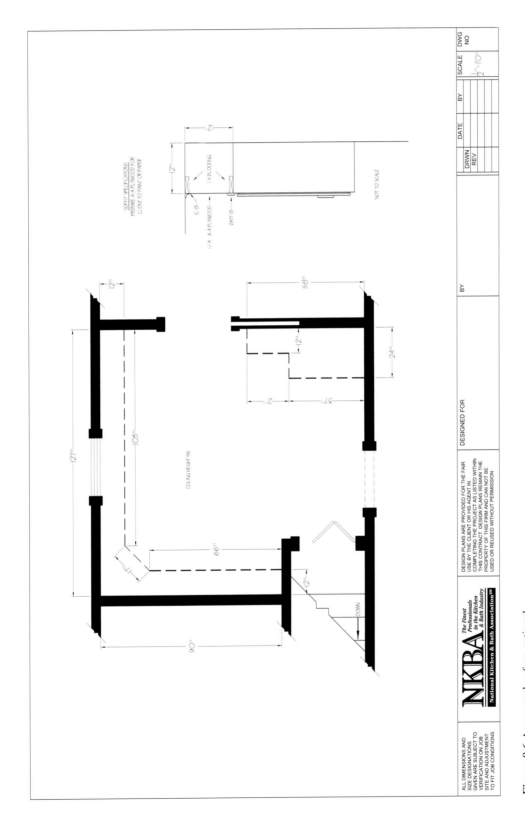

**Figure 8.6** An example of an optional kitchen soffit specifications drawing.

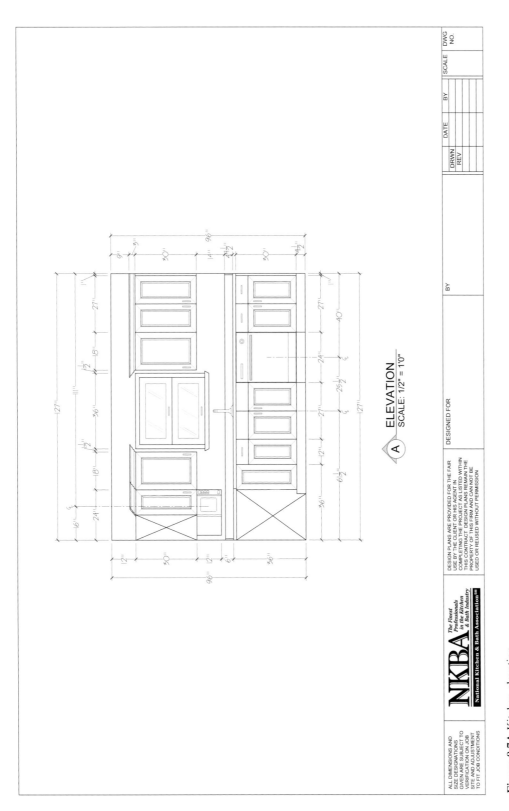

Figure 8.7A Kitchen elevation.

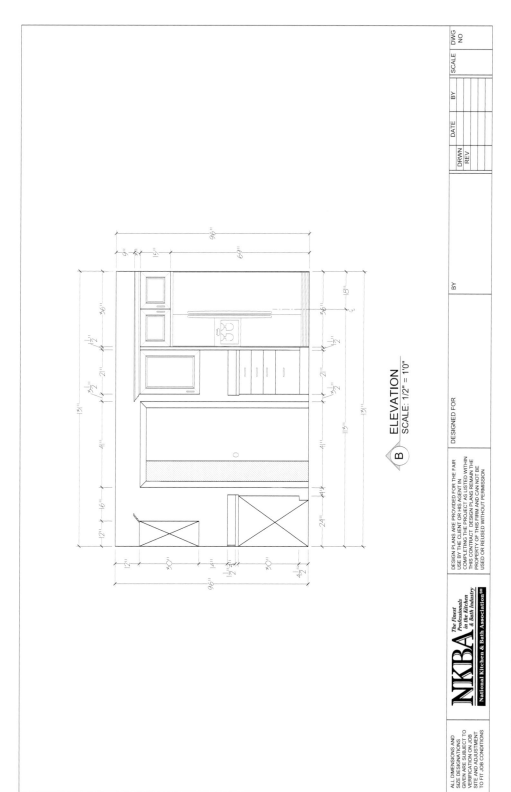

**Figure 8.7B** Kitchen elevation.

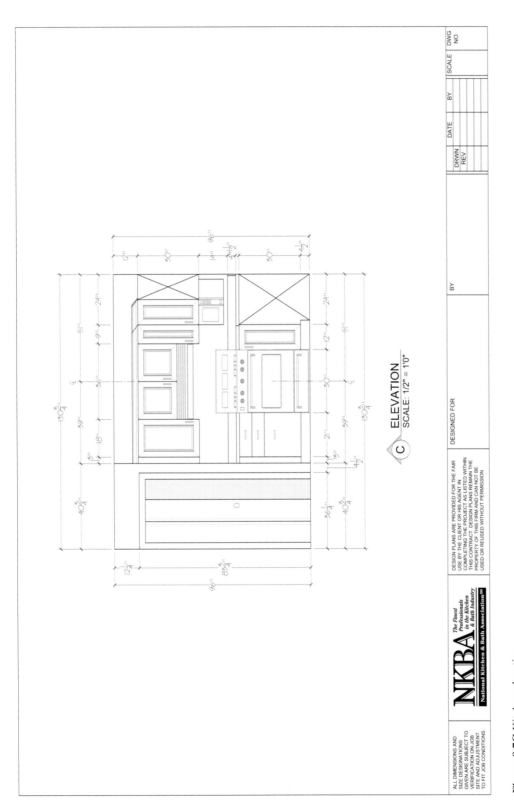

ELEVATION
SCALE: 1/2" = 1'0"

C

**Figure 8.7C** Kitchen elevation.

**Figure 8.8** Kitchen perspective.
(Courtesy of 20-20 Technologies, Inc.)

## SAMPLE DESIGN STATEMENT FOR KITCHEN PROJECT

The client's home was being updated for resale; therefore the project was viewed as a short-term investment. The primary challenge was to create a functional, attractive kitchen in a small space with a limited budget. The clients also requested that the kitchen be separate from the dining area. Most appliances were outdated except for a recently purchased side-by-side refrigerator.

Because of the wall between the dining area and the kitchen, the kitchen would have three openings; an old bi-fold door to the basement, a cased opening into the hall and a new door into the dining room. While necessary, these three openings limit the available space for cabinetry and counter space.

Lighting into the kitchen would be from the small kitchen window and available light from the dining room, but only when the door is open. If the door to the dining area opened into the kitchen it would block some of the cabinetry and counter in an already crowded space.

The lighting was addressed by adding a pocket door between the dining room and the kitchen. This door, when open, would not block any space in the kitchen or dining room.

In addition to the natural lighting, seven recessed lights were added plus under-cabinet task lighting.

The cased opening into the hall was relocated toward the basement door to provide room for cabinets and the refrigerator and allow space for the bi-fold door to open fully. The traffic through the kitchen was minimal since the basement was seldom used and the dining area had a second entrance.

The pocket door behind the cabinets and the refrigerator created a challenge for the required countertop receptacle and mounting for the thirty-inch high wall cabinet. The receptacle was recessed in the side of the base cabinet and mounted in a shallow box to conserve space inside the cabinet. The wall cabinet was mounted to a $1/2"$ plywood panel inset into the $1/2"$ drywall.

The window was small but the only area of interest in the kitchen. To enhance the space, the sink base was extended an extra 3" in depth. The wall cabinets were held away from the small window $1^1/2"$ to produce a compromise between wall cabinet storage and further closing in the window.

Cabinet accessories, crown moulding, laminate counter with wood edging and new appliances helped create the finished look of the new kitchen to increase the beauty and value of the home for a prospective buyer while staying within the client's budget.

## STANDARD SPECIFICATIONS FOR KITCHEN DESIGN AND INSTALLATION PROJECT

# H.H.I.C

687 Willow Grove Street
Hackettstown, NJ 07840

## Standard Specifications for Kitchen Design and Installation

Name: Dr Sara and Jack Blackburn

Home Address: 4540 Mt Vista Lane

City: Hackettstown State: NJ Phone (Home): 908-555-0021

Phone (Office): His: 908-555-4012

Phone (Office): Her: 908-555-7090 Ext 222

Phone (Office): His Pager 908-555-4312

Phone (Jobsite): Same as home

Jobsite Address: Same as above

City: _____ State: _____

By: H.H.I.C.
Hereafter called "Kitchen Specialist"

Kitchen Specialist will supply and deliver only such equipment and material as described in these specifications. Labor connected with this kitchen installation will be supplied by the Kitchen Specialist only as herein specified.

Any equipment, material and labor designated here as "Owner's responsibility" must be furnished and completed by the Owner, or the Owner's Agent in accordance with the work schedule established by the Kitchen Specialist.

Equipment, material and labor not included in these specifications can be supplied by the Kitchen Specialist at an additional cost for which authorization must be given in writing by the Owner, or the Owner's Agent.

All dimension and cabinet designations shown on the floor plan and elevations / interpretive drawings, which are part of these specifications, are subject to adjustments dictated by job conditions.

All surfaces of walls, ceilings, windows and woodwork, except those of factory-made equipment, will be left unpainted or unfinished unless otherwise specified.

If specifications call for re-use of existing equipment, no responsibility on the part of the Kitchen Specialist for appearance, functioning or service shall be implied.

For factory-made equipment, the manufacturer's specifications for quality, design, dimensions, function and installation shall in all cases take precedence over any others.

## Cabinetry

| | Source | | | | |
|---|---|---|---|---|---|
| Key: KS= Kitchen Specialist | Use Existing | Furnished by | | Installed by | |
| O= Owner OA= Owners Agent | ☐Yes ☒No | KS ☒ | O/OA ☐ | KS ☒ | O/OA ☐ |

### Cabinet 1

Manufacturer: Cookville Cabinets

Construction: ☒Frame ☐Frameless

Cabinet Exterior: ☒Wood-Species:Maple    ☐Metal    ☐Decorative Laminate    ☐Other:_____

| Cabinet Exterior Finish: Cinnamon | Cabinet Interior Material: Melamine | Finish: White |
|---|---|---|
| Door Style: Charleston | Hardware: YN-7037901 | |

Special Cabinet Notes: Modification to SB27

### Cabinet 2          ☒ N/A

Manufacturer:

Construction: ☐Frame ☐Frameless

Cabinet Exterior: ☐Wood-Species:_____    ☐Metal    ☐Decorative Laminate    ☐Other:_____

| Cabinet Exterior Finish: | Cabinet Interior Material: | Finish: |
|---|---|---|
| Door Style: | Hardware: | |

Special Cabinet Notes:

## Fascia & Soffit

| | Source | | | | |
|---|---|---|---|---|---|
| Key: KS= Kitchen Specialist | Use Existing | Furnished by | | Installed by | |
| O= Owner OA= Owners Agent | ☐Yes ☐No | KS ☐ | O/OA ☐ | KS ☐ | O/OA ☐ |

### Fascia & Soffit 1

Construction: ☐Flush ☐Extended ☐Recessed ☒Open ☐Remove ☐Other, as per plan:

Finish Material:

Special Fascia / Soffit Notes:

### Fascia & Soffit 2          ☒ N/A

Construction: ☐Flush ☐Extended ☐Recessed ☐Open ☐Remove ☐Other, as per plan:

Finish Material:

Special Fascia / Soffit Notes:

| Countertops | Source | | | | |
|---|---|---|---|---|---|
| Key: KS= Kitchen Specialist | Use Existing | Furnished by | | Installed by | |
| O= Owner OA= Owners Agent | ☐Yes ☒No | KS ☒ | O/OA ☐ | KS ☒ | O/OA ☐ |

**Countertop 1**

Manufacturer: GHI

Material: Laminate                                            Color: #7665

**Design Details**: Deck Thickness _3/4"_ Material _Wood_ Edge Thickness _1/ 1/2"_ Edge Detail/Shape: _Bevel 45 Degree_ Color _Cinnamon_

**Backsplash**: Thickness _3/4"_ Height: _4"_ Color: _Cinnamon_

**End Splash**: Thickness _3/4"_ Height: _4"_ Color: _Cinnamon_

Insert: N/A

**Special Countertop Notes:** Front edge and backsplash to be supplied by Cookville Cabinets. See Countertop Plan for detail. Backsplash and end splashes to be installed after wall covering is installed by owner.

**Countertop 2**          ☒ N/A

Manufacturer:

Material:                                                      Color:

**Design Details**: Deck Thickness___ Material___ Edge Thickness___ Edge Detail/Shape:___ Color___

**Backsplash**: Thickness___ Height:___ Color:___

**End Splash**: Thickness___ Height:___ Color:___

Insert:

**Special Countertop Notes:**

**Countertop 3**          ☒ N/A

Manufacturer:

Material:                                                      Color:

**Design Details**: Deck Thickness___ Material___ Edge Thickness___ Edge Detail/Shape:___ Color___

**Backsplash**: Thickness___ Height:___ Color:___

**End Splash**: Thickness___ Height:___ Color:___

Insert:

**Special Countertop Notes:**

©2006 NKBA BMF14

## Fixtures and Fittings

| Item | Sink # | Brand Name | Model | Finish | Material | Furnished By | | Installed By | | Hooked up By | |
|---|---|---|---|---|---|---|---|---|---|---|---|
| | | | | | | K.S. | O/OA | K.S. | O/OA | K.S. | O/OA |
| Kitchen Sink #1 | 1 | XYZ | 654 | Satin | Stainless | ☒ | ☐ | ☒ | ☐ | ☒ | ☐ |
| No. of Holes | 1 | | | | | ☐ | ☐ | ☐ | ☐ | ☐ | ☐ |
| Faucet #1 | 1 | XYZ | J4110 | Brushed | Chrome | ☒ | ☐ | ☒ | ☐ | ☒ | ☐ |
| Kitchen Sink #2 | N/A | | | | | ☐ | ☐ | ☐ | ☐ | ☐ | ☐ |
| No. of Holes | | | | | | ☐ | ☐ | ☐ | ☐ | ☐ | ☐ |
| Faucet #2 | | | | | | ☐ | ☐ | ☐ | ☐ | ☐ | ☐ |
| Kitchen Sink #3 | N/A | | | | | ☐ | ☐ | ☐ | ☐ | ☐ | ☐ |
| No. of Holes | | | | | | ☐ | ☐ | ☐ | ☐ | ☐ | ☐ |
| Faucet #3 | | | | | | ☐ | ☐ | ☐ | ☐ | ☐ | ☐ |
| Additional Items | | | | | | | | | | | |
| Strainer | 1 | XYZ | ST-67 | Bright | Chrome | ☒ | ☐ | ☒ | ☐ | ☒ | ☐ |
| Hot Water Dispenser | N/A | | | | | ☐ | ☐ | ☐ | ☐ | ☐ | ☐ |
| Chilled Water Dispenser | N/A | | | | | ☐ | ☐ | ☐ | ☐ | ☐ | ☐ |
| Lotion Dispenser | N/A | | | | | ☐ | ☐ | ☐ | ☐ | ☐ | ☐ |
| Water Purifier | 1 | TUA | FW42 US | N/A | N/A | ☒ | ☐ | ☒ | ☐ | ☒ | ☐ |
| Filtered Water Tap | Above | | | | | ☐ | ☐ | ☐ | ☐ | ☐ | ☐ |
| Accessories | | | | | | | | | | | |
| | | | | | | ☐ | ☐ | ☐ | ☐ | ☐ | ☐ |
| | | | | | | ☐ | ☐ | ☐ | ☐ | ☐ | ☐ |
| | | | | | | ☐ | ☐ | ☐ | ☐ | ☐ | ☐ |
| | | | | | | ☐ | ☐ | ☐ | ☐ | ☐ | ☐ |

## Lighting System

| Description | Qty | Location | Model # | Transformer | Finish | Lamp Req. | Furnished By | | Installed By | |
|---|---|---|---|---|---|---|---|---|---|---|
| | | | | | | | K.S. | O/OA | K.S. | O/OA |
| QRS 18" Under Cabinet Fluo | 5 | Per Plan | FL1833 | N/A | White | F15 | ☒ | ☐ | ☒ | ☐ |
| QRS Recessed Ceiling Fixture | 7 | Per Plan | UG78C | N/A | Bright | 60 watt | ☒ | ☐ | ☒ | ☐ |
| | | | | | | | ☐ | ☐ | ☐ | ☐ |
| | | | | | | | ☐ | ☐ | ☐ | ☐ |
| | | | | | | | ☐ | ☐ | ☐ | ☐ |
| | | | | | | | ☐ | ☐ | ☐ | ☐ |

**Special Lighting Notes:**

©2006 NKBA BMF14

## Appliances

| Item | Brand Name | Width | Model | Finish | Fuel | Furnished By | | Installed By | | Hooked up By | |
|---|---|---|---|---|---|---|---|---|---|---|---|
| | | | | | | K.S. | O/OA | K.S. | O/OA | K.S. | O/OA |
| Range | ABC | 30 | 123 | White | Electric | ☒ | ☐ | ☒ | ☐ | ☒ | ☐ |
| Cooktop / Rangetop | N/A | | | | | ☐ | ☐ | ☐ | ☐ | ☐ | ☐ |
| Oven | N/A | | | | | ☐ | ☐ | ☐ | ☐ | ☐ | ☐ |
| Exhaust System A | ABC | 36 | 678 | White | Electric | ☒ | ☐ | ☒ | ☐ | ☒ | ☐ |
| Exhaust System B | N/A | | | | | ☐ | ☐ | ☐ | ☐ | ☐ | ☐ |
| Warming Drawer | N/A | | | | | ☐ | ☐ | ☐ | ☐ | ☐ | ☐ |
| Indoor Grill | N/A | | | | | ☐ | ☐ | ☐ | ☐ | ☐ | ☐ |
| Steam Oven | N/A | | | | | ☐ | ☐ | ☐ | ☐ | ☐ | ☐ |
| Specialty Cooking | N/A | | | | | ☐ | ☐ | ☐ | ☐ | ☐ | ☐ |
| Specialty Cooking | N/A | | | | | ☐ | ☐ | ☐ | ☐ | ☐ | ☐ |
| Specialty Cooking | N/A | | | | | ☐ | ☐ | ☐ | ☐ | ☐ | ☐ |
| Microwave | ABC | 17 | 567 | White | Electric | ☒ | ☐ | ☒ | ☐ | ☐ | ☐ |
| Trim Kit | N/A | | | | | ☐ | ☐ | ☐ | ☐ | ☐ | ☐ |
| Refrigerator #1 | Existing | 34 | | White | Electric | ☐ | ☒ | ☒ | ☐ | ☒ | ☐ |
| Trim Kit | N/A | | | | | ☐ | ☐ | ☐ | ☐ | ☐ | ☐ |
| Refrigerator #2 | N/A | | | | | ☐ | ☐ | ☐ | ☐ | ☐ | ☐ |
| Trim Kit | N/A | | | | | ☐ | ☐ | ☐ | ☐ | ☐ | ☐ |
| Wine / Refrigerator Storage Appliance | N/A | | | | | ☐ | ☐ | ☐ | ☐ | ☐ | ☐ |
| Trim Kit | N/A | | | | | ☐ | ☐ | ☐ | ☐ | ☐ | ☐ |
| Freezer | N/A | | | | | ☐ | ☐ | ☐ | ☐ | ☐ | ☐ |
| Trim Kit | N/A | | | | | ☐ | ☐ | ☐ | ☐ | ☐ | ☐ |
| Ice Maker | Included in Ref. | | N/A | N/A | Electric | ☐ | ☒ | ☒ | ☐ | ☒ | ☐ |
| Trim Kit | N/A | | | | | ☐ | ☐ | ☐ | ☐ | ☐ | ☐ |
| Dishwasher #1 | ABC | 24 | 953 | White | Electric | ☒ | ☐ | ☒ | ☐ | ☒ | ☐ |
| Trim Kit | N/A | | | | | ☐ | ☐ | ☐ | ☐ | ☐ | ☐ |
| Dishwasher #2 | N/A | | | | | ☐ | ☐ | ☐ | ☐ | ☐ | ☐ |
| Trim Kit | N/A | | | | | ☐ | ☐ | ☐ | ☐ | ☐ | ☐ |
| Food Waste Disp.#1 | N/A | | | | | ☐ | ☐ | ☐ | ☐ | ☐ | ☐ |
| Food Waste Disp. #2 | N/A | | | | | ☐ | ☐ | ☐ | ☐ | ☐ | ☐ |
| Compactor | N/A | | | | | ☐ | ☐ | ☐ | ☐ | ☐ | ☐ |
| Trim Kit | N/A | | | | | ☐ | ☐ | ☐ | ☐ | ☐ | ☐ |
| Computer | N/A | | | | | ☐ | ☐ | ☐ | ☐ | ☐ | ☐ |
| Coffee System | N/A | | | | | ☐ | ☐ | ☐ | ☐ | ☐ | ☐ |
| Telephone / Internet | Existing* | | TBD | TBD | | ☐ | ☒ | ☐ | ☒ | ☐ | ☒ |
| Television | N/A | | | | | ☐ | ☐ | ☐ | ☐ | ☐ | ☐ |
| Radio / CD | N/A | | | | | ☐ | ☐ | ☐ | ☐ | ☐ | ☐ |
| VCR / DVD | N/A | | | | | ☐ | ☐ | ☐ | ☐ | ☐ | ☐ |
| Washer | N/A | | | | | ☐ | ☐ | ☐ | ☐ | ☐ | ☐ |
| Dryer | N/A | | | | | ☐ | ☐ | ☐ | ☐ | ☐ | ☐ |
| * KS to locate only | | | | | | ☐ | ☐ | ☐ | ☐ | ☐ | ☐ |

©2006 NKBA BMF14

## Flooring

| Description | Furnished By K.S. | Furnished By O/OA | Installed By K.S. | Installed By O/OA |
|---|---|---|---|---|
| Removal of Existing Floor Covering  Remove existing vinyl | ☒ | ☐ | ☒ | ☐ |
| Remove and Repair Water Damaged Area  None observed | ☐ | ☐ | ☐ | ☐ |
| Preparation of Floor / Subfloor  Prepare for new laminate floor | ☒ | ☐ | ☒ | ☐ |
| Installation of Subfloor Underlayment  Pad as per laminate manufacturer | ☒ | ☐ | ☒ | ☐ |
| New Floor Covering Material Description: | ☒ | ☐ | ☒ | ☐ |
| Manufacturer: JRT  Size: 24" X 48" | ☒ | ☐ | ☒ | ☐ |
| Pattern Number: TS89003  Pattern Name / Repeat: N/A | ☒ | ☐ | ☒ | ☐ |
| Tile Pattern: 12" Square  Grout: N/A | ☒ | ☐ | ☒ | ☐ |

Describe Tile Details:

| Transition / Threshold Treatment  At all entrances. Transition appropriate for flooring in other rooms. | ☒ | ☐ | ☒ | ☐ |
|---|---|---|---|---|

Special Flooring Notes:

## Windows and Doors

| Item | Brand Name | Model | Finish | Hardware | Furnished By K.S. | Furnished By O/OA | Installed By K.S. | Installed By O/OA |
|---|---|---|---|---|---|---|---|---|
| 30" Bi-Fold Door | Pisk Millwork | BF2668 | Cinnamon | Use Existing | ☒ | ☐ | ☒ | ☐ |
| 36" Pocket Door | Pisk Millwork | PD3068 | Cinnamon | BHT-690 | ☒ | ☐ | ☒ | ☐ |
| | | | | | ☐ | ☐ | ☐ | ☐ |
| | | | | | ☐ | ☐ | ☐ | ☐ |
| | | | | | ☐ | ☐ | ☐ | ☐ |
| | | | | | ☐ | ☐ | ☐ | ☐ |

Special Window and Door Notes:  Stain new doors to match cabinet finish (Cinnamon)

## Decorative Surfaces (Wall, Ceiling, Window Materials)

| Description | Material | Color | Finish | Quantity | Furnished By K.S. | Furnished By O/OA | Installed By K.S. | Installed By O/OA |
|---|---|---|---|---|---|---|---|---|
| All walls to be patched and primed | Drywall | N/A | N/A | N/A | ☒ | ☐ | ☒ | ☐ |
| Ceiling to be repaired and primed | Drywall | N/A | N/A | N/A | ☒ | ☐ | ☒ | ☐ |
| Ceiling to be painted | Texture | Cool White | #12 | As needed | ☒ | ☐ | ☒ | ☐ |
| Wall covering by owner TBD* | TBD | TBD | TBD | TBD | ☐ | ☒ | ☐ | ☒ |
| * Material to be determined later. | | | | | ☐ | ☐ | ☐ | ☐ |
| | | | | | ☐ | ☐ | ☐ | ☐ |
| | | | | | ☐ | ☐ | ☐ | ☐ |

Special Decorative Surface Notes:  Wall and ceiling patched, filled, repaired and primed at new wall and old opening. Owner to finish all walls.

## HVAC

| Description  No changes to HVAC System. | Furnished By | | Installed By | |
|---|---|---|---|---|
| | K.S. | O/OA | K.S. | O/OA |
| Ventilation  ABC Hood, Mdl # 678 with 210 cfm | ☒ | ☐ | ☒ | ☐ |
| Rough-In Requirements  Through wall into attic. | ☒ | ☐ | ☒ | ☐ |
| Run New Duct Work for Ventilation System  Duct to outside with roof cap | ☒ | ☐ | ☒ | ☐ |
| Heating  N/A | ☐ | ☐ | ☐ | ☐ |
| Air Conditioning Supply  N/A | ☐ | ☐ | ☐ | ☐ |
| Details: | | | | |

## Electrical Work (except as described above in specific equipment sections)

| Description | Furnished By | | Installed By | |
|---|---|---|---|---|
| | K.S. | O/OA | K.S. | O/OA |
| New Service Panel  Upgrade 150 amp panel to 200 amp | ☒ | ☐ | ☒ | ☐ |
| Code Update  As required | ☒ | ☐ | ☒ | ☐ |

**Details:** Locate new 120v and 240v dedicated circuits per Mechanical Plan. Locate new switches and GFCI receptacles per Mechanical Plan. Locate undercabinet fluorescent lighting and recessed lighting as per Mechanical Plan. Note: Shallow receptacle must be mounted 32" AFF in base cabinet adjacent to refrigerator.

## Plumbing (except as described above in specific equipment sections)

| Description | Furnished By | | Installed By | |
|---|---|---|---|---|
| | K.S. | O/OA | K.S. | O/OA |
| New Rough In Requirements:  Relocate water line for refrigerator. | ☒ | ☐ | ☒ | ☐ |
| | ☐ | ☐ | ☐ | ☐ |
| | ☐ | ☐ | ☐ | ☐ |
| New Drainage Requirements:  N/A | ☐ | ☐ | ☐ | ☐ |
| | ☐ | ☐ | ☐ | ☐ |
| | ☐ | ☐ | ☐ | ☐ |
| New Vent Stack Requirements:  N/A | ☐ | ☐ | ☐ | ☐ |
| | ☐ | ☐ | ☐ | ☐ |
| | ☐ | ☐ | ☐ | ☐ |
| Modifications to Existing Lines:  Plumb sink and dishwasher with new traps, supply lines and shut-offs. | ☒ | ☐ | ☒ | ☐ |
| | ☐ | ☐ | ☐ | ☐ |
| | ☐ | ☐ | ☐ | ☐ |
| Details: | | | | |

## General Carpentry (except as described above in specific equipment sections)

| Description | Furnished By | | Installed By | |
|---|:---:|:---:|:---:|:---:|
| | K.S. | O/OA | K.S. | O/OA |
| **Demolition Work:  Relocate opening in bottom wall.** | | | | |
| Walls-Exterior  N/A | ☐ | ☐ | ☐ | ☐ |
| Walls-Interior  Open wall at new doorway location and fill wall at old location. | ☒ | ☐ | ☒ | ☐ |
| Windows  N/A | ☐ | ☐ | ☐ | ☐ |
| Ceiling  N/A | ☐ | ☐ | ☐ | ☐ |
| Soffit  N/A | ☐ | ☐ | ☐ | ☐ |
| **Existing Fixture and Equipment Removal  By KS** | ☒ | ☐ | ☐ | ☐ |
| **Trash Removal  Arrange for Dumpster in driveway** | ☒ | ☐ | ☒ | ☐ |
| **Reconstruction / Preparation Work (Except as previously stated)** | | | | |
| Windows  N/A | ☐ | ☐ | ☐ | ☐ |
| Doors  Locate Pocket Door in right wall | ☒ | ☐ | ☒ | ☐ |
| Interior Walls  Build new wall between dining room and kitchen. Place header over pocket door location. | ☒ | ☐ | ☒ | ☐ |
| Exterior Wall  N/A | ☐ | ☐ | ☐ | ☐ |
| Soffit / Fascia  N/A | ☐ | ☐ | ☐ | ☐ |
| **HVAC Work:  N/A** | | | | |
| Replace Vents | ☐ | ☐ | ☐ | ☐ |
| Replace Vent Covers  Size:___ | ☐ | ☐ | ☐ | ☐ |
| **Millwork: (Note Cabinetry Installation listed under cabinets)** | | | | |
| Crown Molding  Stain crown molding to match cabinets (Cinnamon) | ☒ | ☐ | ☒ | ☐ |
| Ceiling Details  N/A | ☐ | ☐ | ☐ | ☐ |
| Window / Door Casing  Stain all to match cabinets (Cinnamon) | ☒ | ☐ | ☐ | ☐ |
| Baseboard  Stain all to match cabinets (Cinnamon) | ☒ | ☐ | ☒ | ☐ |
| Wainscoting / Chair Rail  N/A | ☐ | ☐ | ☐ | ☐ |

Details:

## Miscellaneous Work

| Description | Responsibility | |
|---|:---:|:---:|
| | K.S. | O/OA |
| Material Storage Location  Basement | ☒ | ☐ |
| Trash Collection Area  Dumpster in driveway | ☒ | ☐ |
| Trash Removal | ☒ | ☐ |
| Jobsite / Room Cleanup  Broom clean daily | ☒ | ☐ |
| Building Permit (s)  As required | ☒ | ☐ |
| Structural Engineering / Architectural Fees  Required for new wall | ☒ | ☐ |
| Inspection Fees  As required | ☒ | ☐ |
| Jobsite Delivery  To basement | ☒ | ☐ |
| | ☐ | ☐ |
| | ☐ | ☐ |
| | ☐ | ☐ |

©2006 NKBA BMF14

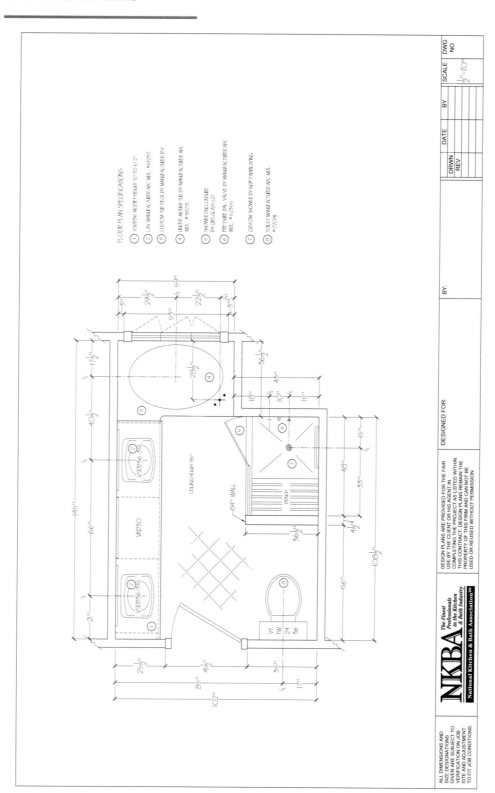

**Figure 8.9** Bathroom floor plan.

See Appendix, page A4 for a fold-out example.

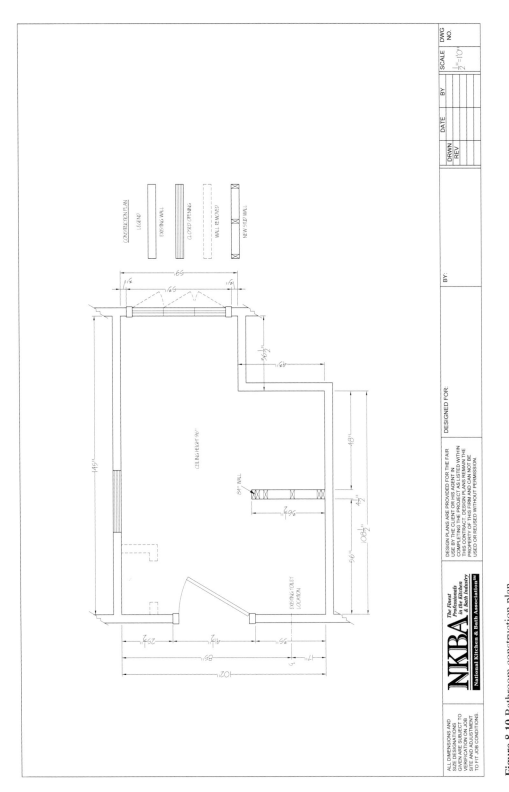

**Figure 8.10** Bathroom construction plan.

See Appendix, page A5 for a fold-out example.

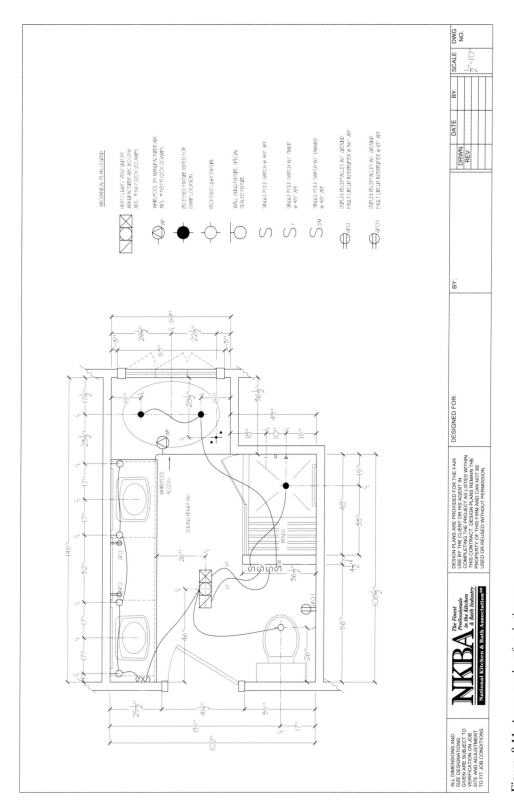

**Figure 8.11** An example of a bathroom mechanical plan.

See Appendix, page A6 for a fold-out example.

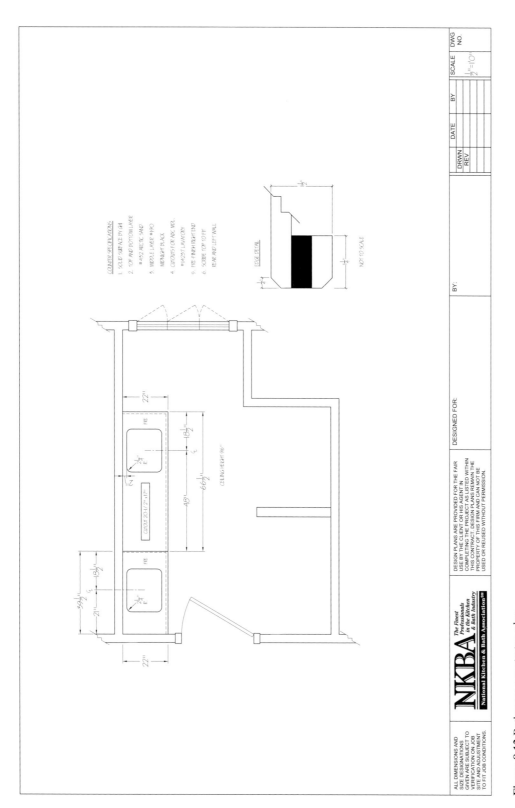

**Figure 8.12** Bathroom countertop plan.

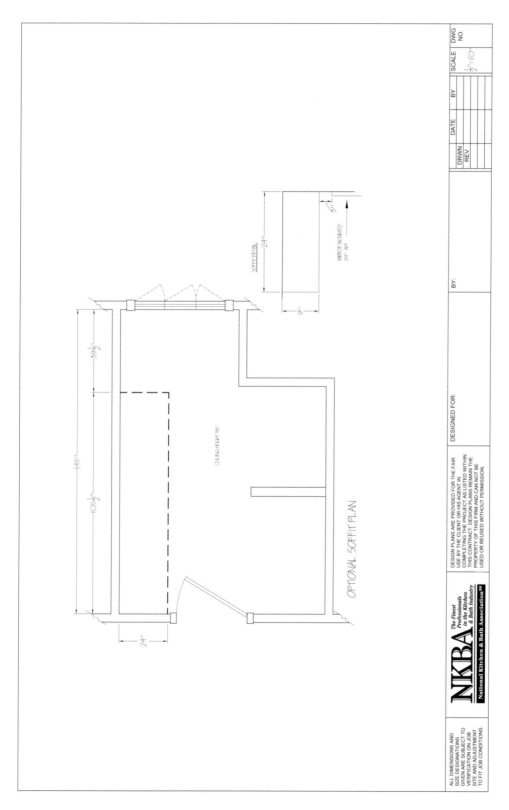

OPTIONAL SOFFIT PLAN

SOFFIT DETAIL

24"

9"

3"

MIRROR MOUNTED
84" AFF

145"

106 1/2"

59 1/2"

24"

CEILING HEIGHT 96"

**NKBA**
*The Finest
Professionals
in the Kitchen
& Bath Industry*℠
**National Kitchen & Bath Association**℠

DESIGNED FOR:

BY:

DRWN
REV

DATE

BY

SCALE
1/2"=1'0"

DWG
NO.

**Figure 8.13** Bathroom soffit plan.

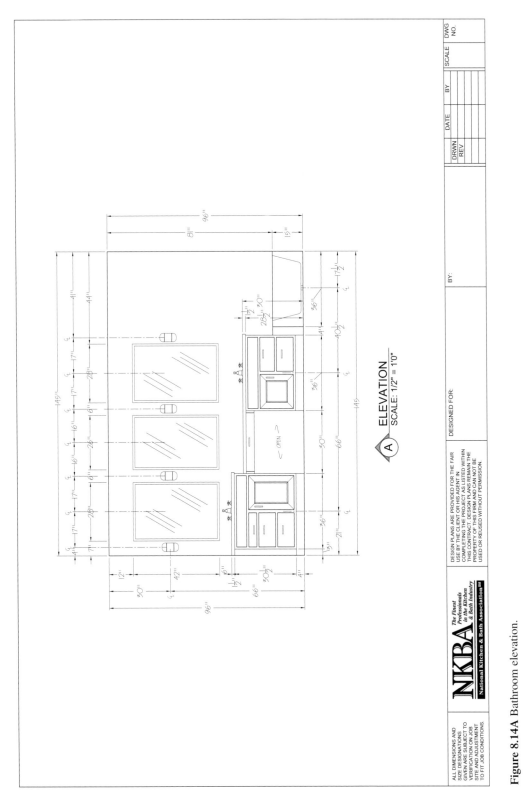

ELEVATION
SCALE: 1/2" = 1'0"

**Figure 8.14A** Bathroom elevation.

DESIGNED FOR:

BY:

DRWN | DATE | BY | SCALE | DWG
REV | | | | NO.

NKBA
The Finest Professionals in the Kitchen & Bath Industry℠
National Kitchen & Bath Association℠

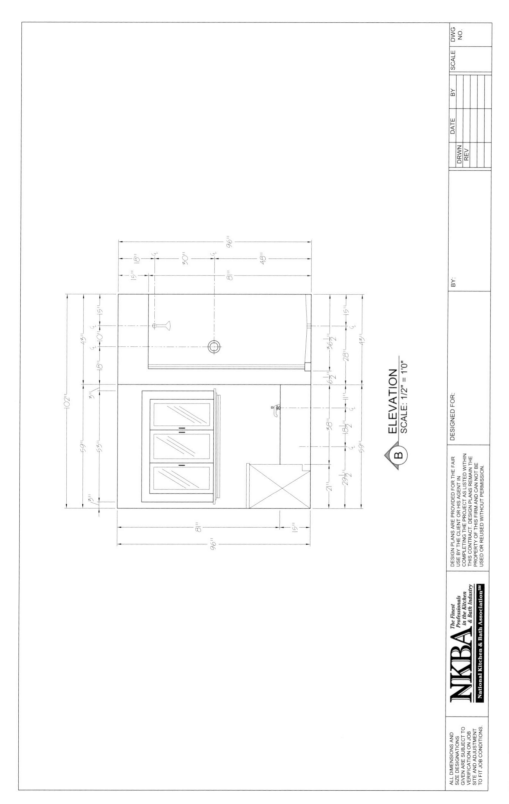

ELEVATION
SCALE: 1/2" = 1'0"

**Figure 8.14B** Bathroom elevation.

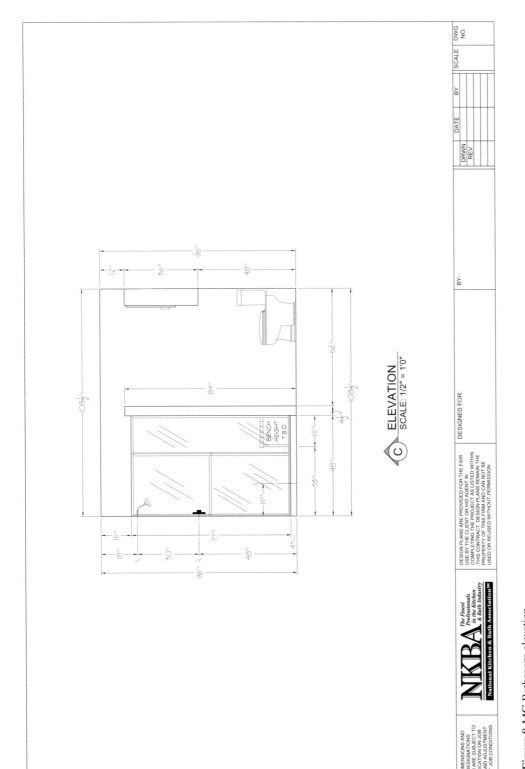

ELEVATION
SCALE: 1/2" = 1'0"

**Figure 8.14C** Bathroom elevation.

DESIGNED FOR:

BY:

DRWN
REV
DATE
BY
SCALE
DWG
NO.

The Finest
Professionals
in the Kitchen
& Bath Industry™
National Kitchen & Bath Association℠

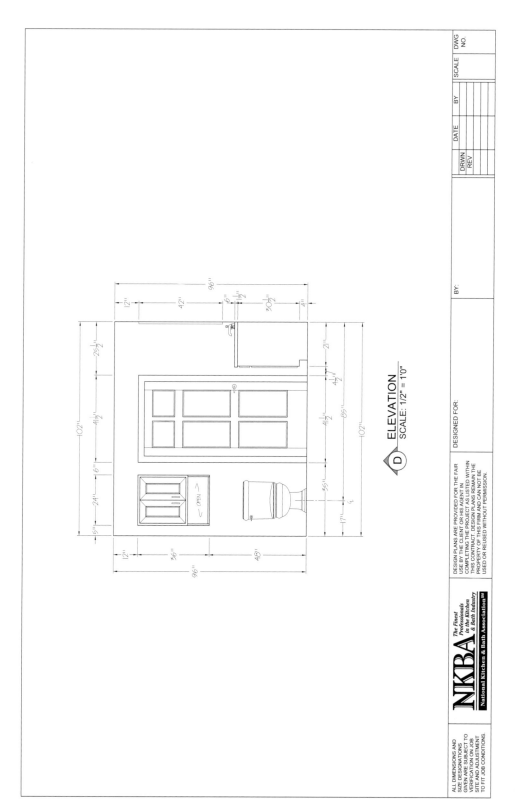

**Figure 8.14D** Bathroom elevation.

**Figure 8.15A** Bathroom perspective.

**Figure 8.15B** Bathroom perspective.

## SAMPLE DESIGN STATEMENT FOR BATHROOM PROJECT

The primary design challenge was to create a master bath for two people of vastly different heights and needs:

- Barbara Smith: 5' 1," likes soaking in the bathtub without disruption, likes to sit while grooming
- Robert Smith: 6' 4," enjoys long, lingering shower that reminds him of his travels
- Empty nesters

The existing space was large but not functional:

- One wall-hung sink for two people of different heights
- Small linen closet
- Concrete slab made major change too expensive
- Toilet must remain in current location

The solution:

- Closed door to former child's bedroom and removed linen closet to create a large continuous counter
- Robert's vanity placed at 36" high
- Barbara's vanity placed at 30" with knee space beneath
- Separate shower and tub meets needs of both clients
- Storage in the vanity cabinets for each person plus additional cabinet above toilet
- Shower pan covers the only changes to the concrete slab
- Client will design a shoji-style screen to provide privacy for the toilet

## STANDARD SPECIFICATIONS
## FOR BATHROOM DESIGN
## AND INSTALLATION PROJECT

# H.H.I.C
687 Willow Grove Street
Hackettstown, NJ 07840

## Standard Specifications for Bathroom Design and Installation

Name: Robert and Barbara Smith

Home Address: 7650 Gatewood Lane

City: Hackettstown            State: NJ            Phone (Home): 908-555-3421

Phone (Office): Her: 908-555-6111

Phone (Office): His cell: 908-555-7792

Phone (Office): N/A

Phone (Jobsite): Same as Home

Jobsite Address: Same as Above

City: _____            State: _____

By: H.H.I.C.

Hereafter called "Bathroom Specialist"

Bathroom Specialist will supply and deliver only such equipment and material as described in these specifications. Labor connected with this Bathroom installation will be supplied by the Bathroom Specialist only as herein specified.

Any equipment, material and labor designated here as "Owner's responsibility" must be furnished and completed by the Owner, or the Owner's Agent in accordance with the work schedule established by the Bathroom Specialist.

Equipment, material and labor not included in these specifications can be supplied by the Bathroom Specialist at an additional cost for which authorization must be given in writing by the Owner, or the Owner's Agent.

All dimension and cabinet designations shown on the floor plan and elevations / interpretive drawings, which are part of these specifications, are subject to adjustments dictated by job conditions.

All surfaces of walls, ceilings, windows and woodwork, except those of factory-made equipment, will be left unpainted or unfinished unless otherwise specified.

If specifications call for re-use of existing equipment, no responsibility on the part of the Bathroom Specialist for appearance, functioning or service shall be implied.

For factory-made equipment, the manufacturer's specifications for quality, design, dimensions, function and installation shall in all cases take precedence over any others.

| Cabinetry | | Source | | | | |
|---|---|---|---|---|---|---|
| Key: BS= Bathroom Specialist<br>O= Owner OA= Owners Agent | | Use Existing<br>☐Yes ☒No | Furnished by<br>BS ☒ | O/OA ☐ | Installed by<br>BS ☒ | O/OA ☐ |

**Cabinet 1**     ☐ N/A

Manufacturer: Cookville Cabinets

Construction: ☒Frame ☐Frameless

Cabinet Exterior: ☒Wood-Species:Maple     ☐Metal ☐Decorative Laminate ☐Other:_____

| Cabinet Exterior Finish: Nutmeg | Cabinet Interior Material: Birch | Finish: Natural |
|---|---|---|
| Door Style: Lexington | Hardware: K-456 | |

Special Cabinet Notes: Modification to height of VSDB36-35L (34 1/2")


**Cabinet 2**     ☒ N/A

Manufacturer:

Construction: ☐Frame ☐Frameless

Cabinet Exterior: ☐Wood-Species:_____     ☐Metal ☐Decorative Laminate ☐Other:_____

| Cabinet Exterior Finish: | Cabinet Interior Material: | Finish: |
|---|---|---|
| Door Style: | Hardware: | |

Special Cabinet Notes:


| Fascia & Soffit | | Source | | | | |
|---|---|---|---|---|---|---|
| Key: BS= Bathroom Specialist<br>O= Owner OA= Owners Agent | | Use Existing<br>☐Yes ☐No | Furnished by<br>BS ☐ | O/OA ☐ | Installed by<br>BS ☐ | O/OA ☐ |

**Fascia & Soffit 1**

Construction: ☐Flush ☐Extended ☐Recessed ☒Open ☐Remove ☐Other, as per plan:

Finish Material: N/A

Special Fascia / Soffit Notes: N/A

OPPTIONAL SOFFIT PLAN AVAILABLE FOR AREA OVER VANITIES ONLY (Note: Not included in estimate.)


**Fascia & Soffit 2**     ☒ N/A

Construction: ☐Flush ☐Extended ☐Recessed ☐Open ☐Remove ☐Other, as per plan:

Finish Material:

Special Fascia / Soffit Notes:

| Surfaces | | | Source | | | | |
|---|---|---|---|---|---|---|---|
| Key: BS= Bathroom Specialist | | Use Existing | Furnished by | | Installed by | | |
| O= Owner OA= Owners Agent | | ☐Yes ☒No | BS ☒ | O/OA ☐ | BS ☒ | O/OA ☐ | |

**Surface 1- Vanity (s)**

Manufacturer: GHI

Material: Solid Surface                    Color: Artic Sand (#432) and Mid-Night Black (#190)

Design Details: Deck Thickness 1/2 " Material S/S Edge Thickness 1 1/2" Edge Detail Shape Beveled Color See Below

Backsplash: Thickness_N/A Height:___ Color:___

End Splash: Thickness_N/A Height:___ Color:___

Insert: N/A

Special Notes: Top and bottom layer of front edge is to be Artic Sand. Middle layer to be Mid-Night Black. 1/4 " bevel edge top and bottom. Drop-in lavs by ABC Model #14237

**Surface 2- Tub / Deck / Surround**

Manufacturer: RST

Material: Solid Surface

Design Details: Deck Thickness 1/2" Material S/S Edge Thickness 1/2" Edge Detail Shape Square Color Artic Sand (#432)

Wall Backsplash: Thickness_N/A Height:___ Color:___

End Splash: Thickness_N/A Height:___ Color:___

Insert: N/A

Special Notes: RST is to build custom Bath Deck using Solid Surface Material Provided by GHI. Deck designed to contain undermount tub by ABC Model #38771

**Surface 3- Shower Surround**

Manufacturer: NOP

Material: Solid Surface

Design Details: Deck Thickness 1/2" Material S/S Edge Thickness 1/2" Edge Detail Shape Square Color Artic Sand (#432)

Backsplash: Thickness_N/A Height:___ Color:___

End Splash: Thickness_N/A Height:___ Color:___

Insert: Shower bench to be inlay strips of Mid-Night Black (#190)

Special Notes: NOP to supply drawing for shower area. Final drawing to be approved by B.S and Owner. Tempered Glass Enclosure by QRS Glass Company.

**Surface 4 - Other**          ☒ N/A

Manufacturer:

Material:

Design Details: Deck Thickness        Material        Edge Thickness        Edge Detail Shape        Color

Backsplash: Thickness___ Height:___ Color:___

End Splash: Thickness___ Height:___ Color:___

Insert:

©2006 NKBA BMF14

Special Notes:

## Bath Fixtures & Fittings - Water Closet

| Use Existing | Furnished by | | Installed by | |
|---|---|---|---|---|
| ☐Yes ☒No | BS ☒ | O/OA ☐ | BS ☒ | O/OA ☐ |

| | Brand Name | Model | Configuration | Color / Finish |
|---|---|---|---|---|
| ☒ Round | ABC | 77041 | C/C | Sand |
| ☐ Elongated | | | | |
| ☐ Soft | | | | |
| ☐ Low Profile | | | | |
| Trip Lever | ABC | 71342C | Std | Chrome |
| Stop and Supply | ABC | 71551C & 71820C | Std | Chrome |
| Height | Existing | N/A | N/A | N/A |

## Bath Fixtures & Fittings - Bidet / Bidet Seat

| Use Existing | Furnished by | | Installed by | |
|---|---|---|---|---|
| ☐Yes ☐No ☒N/A | BS ☐ | O/OA ☐ | BS ☐ | O/OA ☐ |

| | Brand Name | Model | Configuration | Color / Finish |
|---|---|---|---|---|
| Fittings | | | | |
| Vacuum Breaker | | | | |
| Miscellaneous | | | | |

## Bath Fixtures & Fittings - Bathtub

| Use Existing | Furnished by | | Installed by | |
|---|---|---|---|---|
| ☐Yes ☒No | BS ☒ | O/OA ☐ | BS ☒ | O/OA ☐ |

| | Brand Name | Model | Configuration | Color / Finish |
|---|---|---|---|---|
| Bathtub | ABC Undermount Tub | 38771 | Oval | Sand |
| Fitting #1 | ABC | 72310C | 8" Spread | Chrome |
| Fitting #2 | N/A | | | |
| Fitting #3 | N/A | | | |
| Waste and Overflow | ABC | 74571C | | Chrome |
| Stop and Supply | TRS | P4355 | | N/A |
| Miscellaneous | | | | |
| Size | | | | |

## Bath Fixtures & Fittings – Jetted Bathtub System

| Use Existing | Furnished by | | Installed by | |
|---|---|---|---|---|
| ☐Yes ☒No | BS ☒ | O/OA ☐ | BS ☒ | O/OA ☐ |

| | Brand Name | Model | Configuration | Color / Finish |
|---|---|---|---|---|
| ☒Air Jets | ABC | Included with tub | Standard | Sand |
| ☐Adjustable Whirlpool Jets | | | | |
| ☐Massage Whirlpool Jets | | | | |
| Chromatherapy System | | | | |
| Fittings | | | | |
| Miscellaneous | Access: Left Front Bottom | | | |

©2006 NKBA BMF14

## Bath Fixtures & Fittings - Shower

| Use Existing | Furnished by | | Installed by | |
|---|---|---|---|---|
| ☐Yes ☒No | BS ☒ | O/OA ☐ | BS ☒ | O/OA ☐ |

| | Brand Name | Model | Configuration | Color / Finish |
|---|---|---|---|---|
| Pan | NOP | Custom | Rectangular | Artic Sand |
| Curb | " | " | N/A | Artic Sand |
| Seat / Bench | " | " | Box | Artic Sand/Mid-Night Black Strips |
| Shelf / Recess | N/A | | | |
| Drain | TRS | C4100 | N/A | Chrome |
| Fittings | ABC | #52355 | N/A | Chrome |
| Shower #1 | ABC | #64700C | N/A | Chrome |
| Shower #2 | N/A | | | |
| Shower #3-Body Spray | N/A | | | |
| Shower #4- Hand-Held | N/A | | | |
| Stop & Supply | TRS | P4571C | N/A | N/A |
| Shower Floor | NOP | Custom | Slope to drain | Artic Sand |
| Drapery Rod | N/A | | | |
| Shower Drapery | N/A | | | |

## Bath Fixtures & Fittings – Lavatory 1

| Use Existing | Furnished by | | Installed by | |
|---|---|---|---|---|
| ☐Yes ☒No | BS ☒ | O/OA ☐ | BS ☒ | O/OA ☐ |

| | Brand Name | Model | Configuration | Color / Finish |
|---|---|---|---|---|
| Type: | | | | |
| ☐ Under-mount | | | | |
| ☒ Top Mount | ABC | #14237 | Rectangular w/ Oval Bowl | Sand |
| ☐ Vessel | | | | |
| ☐ Pedestal | | | | |
| ☐ Integral | | | | |
| Fittings | ABC | #56302C | Std. | Chrome |
| Drilling Spread | N/A | N/A | 4" Spread | N/A |
| Stop & Supply | TRS | P4571C | N/A | Chrome |
| Pedestal Trap Cover | | | | |
| Miscellaneous | | | | |

## Bath Fixtures & Fittings – Lavatory 2

| Use Existing | Furnished by | | Installed by | |
|---|---|---|---|---|
| ☐Yes ☒No ☐N/A | BS ☒ | O/OA ☐ | BS ☒ | O/OA ☐ |

| | Brand Name | Model | Configuration | Color / Finish |
|---|---|---|---|---|
| ☐ Under-mount | | | | |
| ☐ Top Mount | Same as Above | | | |
| ☐ Vessel | | | | |
| ☐ Pedestal | | | | |
| ☐ Integral | | | | |
| Fittings | Same as Above | | | |
| Drilling Spread | Same as Above | | | |
| Stop & Supply | Same as Above | | | |
| Pedestal Trap Cover | | | | |
| Miscellaneous | | | | |

## Bath Fixtures & Fittings – Steam Bath

| Use Existing | Furnished by | | Installed by | |
|---|---|---|---|---|
| ☐Yes ☐No ☒N/A | BS ☐ | O/OA ☐ | BS ☐ | O/OA ☐ |

| | Brand Name | Model | Configuration | Color / Finish |
|---|---|---|---|---|
| Steam Enclosure Materials | | | | |
| Steam Generator | | | | |
| Steam Outlet Control | | | | |
| Miscellaneous | | | | |

## Bath Fixtures & Fittings – Sauna

| Use Existing | Furnished by | | Installed by | |
|---|---|---|---|---|
| ☐Yes ☐No ☒N/A | BS ☐ | O/OA ☐ | BS ☐ | O/OA ☐ |

| | Brand Name | Model | Configuration | Color / Finish |
|---|---|---|---|---|
| Interior Materials | | | | |
| Heater | | | | |
| Control | | | | |
| Miscellaneous | | | | |

## Bath Fixtures & Fittings – Exercise Equipment

| Use Existing | Furnished by | | Installed by | |
|---|---|---|---|---|
| ☐Yes ☐No ☒N/A | BS ☐ | O/OA ☐ | BS ☐ | O/OA ☐ |

| | Brand Name | Model | Configuration | Color / Finish |
|---|---|---|---|---|
| N/A | | | | |
| | | | | |
| | | | | |
| | | | | |

## Bath Fixtures & Fittings – Miscellaneous

| Use Existing | Furnished by | | Installed by | |
|---|---|---|---|---|
| ☐Yes ☐No | BS ☐ | O/OA ☐ | BS ☐ | O/OA ☐ |

| | Brand Name | Model | Configuration | Color / Finish |
|---|---|---|---|---|
| | | | | |
| | | | | |
| | | | | |

## Accessories (as per approved drawing)

| Use Existing | Furnished by | | Installed by | |
|---|---|---|---|---|
| ☐Yes ☒No | BS ☒ | O/OA ☒ | BS ☒ | O/OA ☐ |

| Item | Qty | Brand Name | Model | Size | Color / Finish |
|---|---|---|---|---|---|
| Mirror #1 | 2 | Custom by BS | Custom | 28" x 42" High | Frame to match cabinetry |
| Mirror #2 | 1 | Custom by BS | Custom | 26" x 42" High | Frame to match cabinetry |
| Medicine Cabinet | N/A | | | | |
| Glass Shelves | N/A | | | | |
| Towel Bar | TBD* | Owner will supply | | | |
| Hydronic / Electric | N/A | | | | |
| Towel Ring | TBD* | Owner will supply | | | |
| Robe Hook | TBD* | Owner will supply | | | |
| Tub Soap Dish | TBD* | Owner will Supply | | | |
| Shower Soap Dish | TBD* | Owner will supply | | | |
| Bidet Soap Dish | N/A | | | | |
| Lavatory Soap Dish | N/A | | | | |
| Grab Bar | 2 | UHM | #C84-30 | 30" | Sand |
| Paper Holder | 1 | Free Standing/Owner will supply | | | |
| Magazine Rack | N/A | | | | |
| Soap / Lotion Dispenser | N/A | | | | |
| Tumbler Holder | N/A | | | | |
| Tissue Holder | N/A | | | | |
| Scale | N/A | | | | |
| Toothbrush Holder | N/A | | | | |
| Hamper | N/A | | | | |
| Toilet Tank Cabinet | 1 | Cookville Cabinets | VTTW2436 | 24" x 36" | Maple (Nutmeg) |
| *TBD (To Be Determined) | | Owner will Select and Supply | | | |

©2006 NKBA BMF14

## Closet Specifications

| Use Existing | Furnished by | | Installed by | |
|---|---|---|---|---|
| ☐Yes ☐No ☒N/A | BS ☐ | O/OA ☐ | BS ☐ | O/OA ☐ |

| Item | Brand Name | Model | Size | Color / Finish |
|---|---|---|---|---|
| Poles | N/A | | | |
| Shelves | | | | |
| Drawers | | | | |
| Shoe Racks | | | | |
| Belt / Tie /Scarf Racks | | | | |
| Safe | | | | |
| Ironing Board | | | | |
| Pull Down Units | | | | |
| | | | | |
| | | | | |

## Lighting System

| Description | Qty | Location | Model # | Transformer | Finish | Lamp Req. | Furnished B.S. | O/OA | Installed By B.S. | O/OA |
|---|---|---|---|---|---|---|---|---|---|---|
| Keys, Moisture Proof Recessed | 1 | Shower | K435 | N/A | Chrome | 60 watt | ☒ | ☐ | ☒ | ☐ |
| Keys, Moisture Proof Recessed | 2 | Tub | K435 | N/A | Chrome | 60 watt | ☒ | ☐ | ☒ | ☐ |
| Spartin * | 4 | Lav Wall | U7P36 | N/A | Chrome | 60 watt | ☒ | ☐ | ☒ | ☐ |
| Keys, Recessed | 1 | Toilet | K706 | N/A | Chrome | 60 watt | ☒ | ☐ | ☒ | ☐ |
| ABC (Heat/Light/Vent) | 1 | Per Plan | #567 | N/A | Chrome | 60 watt | ☒ | ☐ | ☒ | ☐ |

**Special Lighting Notes:** The Spartin Fixtures listed are for outdoor use and are sealed fixtures. Suggested because of proximity to bathtub.

## Flooring

| Description | Furnished By B.S. | O/OA | Installed By B.S. | O/OA |
|---|---|---|---|---|
| Hazardous Waste Removal (Asbestos)  None Observed To Be Determined (TBD) | ☐ | ☐ | ☐ | ☐ |
| Removal of Existing Floor Covering | ☒ | ☐ | ☒ | ☐ |
| Remove and Repair Water Damaged Area  None Observed TBD | ☒ | ☐ | ☒ | ☐ |
| Preparation of Floor / Subfloor   See Below | ☒ | ☐ | ☒ | ☐ |
| Installation of Subfloor Underlayment  Backer Board TM Installed Over Subfloor | ☒ | ☐ | ☒ | ☐ |
| New Floor Covering Material Description: | ☒ | ☐ | ☐ | ☐ |
| Manufacturer:  KLM TILE CO.           Size: 9" | ☒ | ☐ | ☒ | ☐ |
| Pattern Number: 56300           Pattern Name / Repeat:  N/A | ☒ | ☐ | ☒ | ☐ |
| Tile Pattern:  COSTAL           Grout:  G14-2 | ☒ | ☐ | ☒ | ☐ |

**Describe Tile Details:**   PLACE DIAGONAL

| Transition / Threshold Treatment | ☒ | ☐ | ☒ | ☐ |
|---|---|---|---|---|

**Special Flooring Notes:**  FILL AND LEVEL AT OLD CLOSET LOCATION. CHECK FOR WATER DAMAGE AFTER TEAROUT. REPAIR AS NEEDED.

NO INDICATION OF ASBESTOS FLOORING. TO BE DETERMINED DURING EXISTING FLOOR REMOVAL.

## Windows and Doors

| Item | Brand Name | Model | Finish | Hardware | Furnished By | | Installed By | |
|---|---|---|---|---|---|---|---|---|
| | | | | | B.S. | O/OA | B.S. | O/OA |
| BATH ENTRY DOOR | PISK MILLWORK | 30RH-74 | MATCH TRIM | KUT #35001 | ☒ | ☐ | ☒ | ☐ |
| | | | | | ☐ | ☐ | ☐ | ☐ |
| | | | | | ☐ | ☐ | ☐ | ☐ |
| | | | | | ☐ | ☐ | ☐ | ☐ |
| | | | | | ☐ | ☐ | ☐ | ☐ |
| | | | | | ☐ | ☐ | ☐ | ☐ |

**Casing** Size: 2 1/4 Style: #1004

**Special Window and Door Notes:** REMOVE AND CLOSE OPENING AT DOOR TO BEDROOM #3

## Decorative Surfaces (Wall, Ceiling, Window Materials)

| Description | Material | Color | Finish | Quantity | Furnished By | | Installed By | |
|---|---|---|---|---|---|---|---|---|
| | | | | | B.S. | O/OA | B.S. | O/OA |
| PATCH AND PRIME ALL WALLS | DRYWALL | N/A | PAINT READY | N/A | ☒ | ☐ | ☒ | ☐ |
| PATCH AND PRIME CEILING AS NEEDED | DRYWALL | N/A | LIGHT BEAD | N/A | ☒ | ☐ | ☒ | ☐ |
| PAINT WALLS AND CEILING | TBD | TBD | TBD | TBD | ☐ | ☒ | ☐ | ☒ |
| WINDOW TREATMENTS | TBD | TBD | TBD | TBD | ☐ | ☒ | ☐ | ☒ |
| | | | | | ☐ | ☐ | ☐ | ☐ |

**Special Decorative Surface Notes:** FILL AND PATCH AT WALL AND CEILING OF OLD CLOSET. FILL AND PATCH WALL ON BOTH SIDES AT OLD DOOR OPENING TO BEDROOM #3. DRYWALL, TAPE AND FINISH NEW WALL AT SHOWER. BS TO PRIME WALLS ONLY. OWNER TO PAINT.

## HVAC

| Description | Furnished By | | Installed By | |
|---|---|---|---|---|
| | B.S. | O/OA | B.S. | O/OA |
| Ventilation No Changes Required For HVAC System | ☐ | ☐ | ☐ | ☐ |
| Rough-In Requirements | ☐ | ☐ | ☐ | ☐ |
| Run New Duct Work for Ventilation System New Duct Work For Heat/Light/Vent System | ☒ | ☐ | ☒ | ☐ |
| Heating | ☐ | ☐ | ☐ | ☐ |
| Air Conditioning Supply | ☐ | ☐ | ☐ | ☐ |

**Details:** NO CHANGES TO CEILING MOUNTED DUCTS. TIMED SWITCH FOR VENT FAN.

## Electrical Work (except as described above in specific equipment sections)

| Description | Furnished By | | Installed By | |
|---|---|---|---|---|
| | B.S. | O/OA | B.S. | O/OA |
| New Service Panel No Changes Required For Existing 200amp Panel | ☐ | ☐ | ☐ | ☐ |
| Code Update As Required | ☒ | ☐ | ☒ | ☐ |
| Wiring for Heated Tile Floor N/A | ☐ | ☐ | ☐ | ☐ |

**Details:** ADD NEW CIRCUIT FOR WHIRLPOOL AND HEAT/VENT/LIGHT. VERIFY ALL BATH RECEPTACLES ARE GFCI PROTECTED. ADD LIGHTING, SWITCHES AND RECEPTACLES AS PER MECHANICAL PLAN.

©2006 NKBA BMF14

## Plumbing (except as described above in specific equipment sections)

| Description | Furnished By | | Installed By | |
|---|---|---|---|---|
| | B.S. | O/OA | B.S. | O/OA |
| **New Rough In Requirements:** RELOCATE LAVATORIES TO TOP WALL. RELOCATE TUB SUPPLY LINES. NEW SUPPLY LINES FOR SHOWER. | ☒ | ☐ | ☒ | ☐ |
| | ☐ | ☐ | ☐ | ☐ |
| | ☐ | ☐ | ☐ | ☐ |
| **New Drainage Requirements** NEW DRAINS FOR LAVATORIES AND SHOWER. REWORK EXISTING TUB DRAIN. | ☒ | ☐ | ☒ | ☐ |
| | ☐ | ☐ | ☐ | ☐ |
| | ☐ | ☐ | ☐ | ☐ |
| **New Vent Stack Requirements:** NEW VENT STACK REQUIRED FOR LAVATORIES AND SHOWER LOCATIONS. | ☒ | ☐ | ☒ | ☐ |
| | ☐ | ☐ | ☐ | ☐ |
| | ☐ | ☐ | ☐ | ☐ |
| **Modifications to Existing Lines:** AS REQUIRED PER PLAN. | ☒ | ☐ | ☒ | ☐ |
| | ☐ | ☐ | ☐ | ☐ |
| | ☐ | ☐ | ☐ | ☐ |

**Details:** ANY OPENINGS IN WALL FOR PLUMBING MODIFICATIONS WILL BE FINISHED AND PRIMED BY BS WITH PAINT BY OWNER.

## General Carpentry (except as described above in specific equipment sections)

| Description | Furnished By | | Installed By | |
|---|---|---|---|---|
| | B.S. | O/OA | B.S. | O/OA |
| **Demolition Work:** | | | | |
| Walls-Exterior N/A | ☐ | ☐ | ☐ | ☐ |
| Walls-Interior Remove Old Closet | ☒ | ☐ | ☒ | ☐ |
| Windows/Doors Remove Door to Bedroom #3 | ☒ | ☐ | ☒ | ☐ |
| Ceiling N/A | ☐ | ☐ | ☐ | ☐ |
| Soffit N/A | ☐ | ☐ | ☐ | ☐ |
| **Existing Fixture and Equipment Removal** | ☒ | ☐ | ☒ | ☐ |
| **Trash Removal** To Container in Driveway | ☒ | ☐ | ☒ | ☐ |
| **Reconstruction / Preparation Work (Except as Previously Stated)** N/A | | | | |
| Windows | ☐ | ☐ | ☐ | ☐ |
| Doors | ☐ | ☐ | ☐ | ☐ |
| Interior Walls | ☐ | ☐ | ☐ | ☐ |
| Exterior Wall | ☐ | ☐ | ☐ | ☐ |
| Soffit / Fascia | ☐ | ☐ | ☐ | ☐ |
| **HVAC Work:** N/A | | | | |
| Replace Vents | ☐ | ☐ | ☐ | ☐ |
| Replace Vent Covers Size:_____ | ☐ | ☐ | ☐ | ☐ |
| **Millwork: (Note Cabinetry Installation listed under cabinets)** | | | | |
| Crown Molding N/A | ☐ | ☐ | ☐ | ☐ |
| Ceiling Details N/A | ☐ | ☐ | ☐ | ☐ |
| Window / Door Casing All Trim Stained To Match Cabinetry | ☒ | ☐ | ☒ | ☐ |
| Baseboard Stained To Match Cabinetry | ☒ | ☐ | ☒ | ☐ |
| Wainscotting / Chair Rail N/A | ☐ | ☐ | ☐ | ☐ |

**Details:**

## Miscellaneous Work

| Description | Responsibility | |
|---|---|---|
| | B.S. | O/OA |
| Material Storage Location  Cabinetry in Garage, Right Side | ☒ | ☐ |
| Trash Collection Area  BS To Arrange for Container in Driveway, Right Side. | ☒ | ☐ |
| Trash Removal  Daily to Container | ☒ | ☐ |
| Jobsite / Room Cleanup  Broom Clean Daily | ☒ | ☐ |
| Building Permit (s)  As Required | ☒ | ☐ |
| Structural Engineering / Architectural Fees  N/A | ☐ | ☐ |
| Inspection Fees  As Required | ☒ | ☐ |
| Jobsite Delivery  To Garage and Storage Container* | ☒ | ☐ |
| *On Site Storage Container for items that will not fit in garage. Between garage and trash container. | ☒ | ☐ |
| | ☐ | ☐ |
| | ☐ | ☐ |

# Chapter 9: Converting to the Metric System

**METRIC CONVERSION CHART**

Kitchen and bathroom drawings in the United States should be drawn to a scale of $^1/2$" inch equals one foot ($^1/2$" = 1'-0"). However, in most of the world, the metric system has replaced the imperial system of measuring. When using the metric system to draft kitchen and bathroom drawings, a scale of 1cm to 20cm should be used. Typically, plans will show the scale as 1:20.

It is important to note that an exact conversion will result in incorrect measurements. In areas where the metric system is used, kitchen and bath products will be listed in metric sizes, which will not be the same as converting imperial to metric.

Example: United States cabinet manufacturers typically build cabinets in 3 inch increments. Countries using the metric system build cabinets in increments of 5 and 10 cm. Therefore if you are planning a 12 inch or 18 inch cabinet using metric dimensions your "hard" conversion to metric would be 30.48cm or 45.72cm. However, the actual cabinet size would be 30cm or 45cm respectively.

For more information on typical metric cabinet sizing, refer to the *Kitchen & Bath Products* book, part of NKBA's *Professional Resource Library*.

The following chart can be used when converting from imperial to metric measurements.

| | Inches | Centimeters |
|---|---|---|
| Actual metric conversion to millimeters is 1'' = 25.4mm. To facilitate conversions between imperial and metric dimensioning for calculations under 1,'' 24mm is used. | 1/8 | .32 |
| | 1/4 | .64 |
| | 1/2 | 1.27 |
| | 3/4 | 1.91 |
| | 1 | 2.54 |
| To facilitate conversions between imperial and metric for calculations over 1,'' 25mm is typically used. | 3 | 7.62 |
| Actual imperial conversion to centimeters is 1'' = 2.54cm. | 6 | 15.24 |
| | 9 | 22.86 |
| | 12 | 30.48 |
| | 15 | 38.1 |
| | 18 | 45.72 |
| | 21 | 53.34 |
| | 24 | 60.96 |
| | 27 | 68.58 |
| | 30 | 76.2 |
| | 33 | 83.82 |
| | 36 | 91.44 |
| | 39 | 99.06 |
| | 42 | 106.68 |
| | 45 | 114.3 |
| | 48 | 122.00 |
| | 51 | 129.54 |
| | 54 | 137.16 |
| | 57 | 144.78 |
| | 60 | 152.4 |
| | 63 | 160.02 |
| | 66 | 167.64 |
| | 69 | 175.26 |
| | 72 | 182.88 |
| | 75 | 190.5 |
| | 78 | 198.12 |
| | 81 | 205.74 |
| | 84 | 213.36 |
| | 87 | 220.98 |
| | 90 | 228.6 |
| | 93 | 236.22 |
| | 96 | 243.84 |
| | 99 | 251.46 |
| | 102 | 259.08 |
| | 105 | 266.7 |
| | 108 | 274.32 |
| | 111 | 281.94 |
| | 114 | 289.56 |
| | 117 | 297.18 |
| | 120 | 304.8 |
| | 123 | 312.42 |
| | 126 | 320.04 |
| | 129 | 327.66 |
| | 132 | 327.66 |
| | 135 | 342.9 |
| | 138 | 350.52 |
| | 141 | 358.14 |
| | 144 | 365.76 |

## METRIC EQUIVALENTS

### Length

10 millimeters = 1 centimeter (CM)

10 centimeters = 1 decimeter

10 decimeters = 1 meter (M)

10 meters = 1 dekameter

100 meters = 1 hectometer

1000 meters = 1 kilometer (KM)

### Linear Drawing Measurements

1 millimeter = .03937"

1 centimeter = .3937"

1 meter = 39.37"


1" = 25.4MM

1" = 2.54CM

1" = .0254M


12" = 304.8MM

12" = 30.48CM

12" = .3048M

### Dry Measure

1 pint = .550599 liter

1 quart = 1.101197 liter

1 peck = 8.80958 liter

1 bushel = .35238 hectoliter

### Liquid Measure

1 pint = .473167 liter

1 quart = .946332 liter

1 gallon = 3.785329 liter

## Area

100 sq. millimeters = 1 sq. centimeter

100 sq. centimeters = 1 sq. decimeter

100 sq. decimeters = 1 sq. meter

100 sq. meters = 1 acre

10,000 sq. meters = 1 hectare

100 hectares = 1 sq. kilometer

## Square Measure

1 sq. inch = 6.4516 sq. centimeters

1 sq. foot = 9.29034 sq. decimeters

1 sq. yard = .836131 sq. meter

1 acre = .40469 hectare

1 sq. mile = 2.59 sq. kilometers

## Cubic Measure

1 cubic inch = 16.3872 cubic centimeters

1 cubic foot = .028318 cubic meters

1 cubic yard = .76456 cubic meters

## Long Measure

1 inch = 25.4 millimeters

1 foot = .3 meter

1 yard = .914401 meter

1 mile = 1.609347 kilometers

# CHAPTER 10: Closing Comment

Communication has been and always will be one of the most important aspects of any business. The ability to convey your thoughts and ideas to those around you is vitally important.

By studying and mastering the information in this book, you will become fluent in a new language: the language of Design Presentation. Keep in mind that most designers, architects, builders, electricians and plumbers all speak the same language. Any of these professionals should be able to look at a well documented plan and complete their area of responsibility in order to see the entire project through to completion. It is your responsibility as a kitchen or bath designer to recognize and comprehend the common language all related professionals understand.

Each one of us will have our own unique style in the layout and presentation of our ideas. But we must meet the drafting standards recognized by others in the industry to be successful in eliminating costly errors associated with misread plans.

Your skills will continue to develop through practice and soon you will have your own style. This creative journey through which you develop skillful drafting techniques is rewarding. However, what will be most rewarding is when your ideas become reality through the creation of professional kitchen and bathroom design documents.

Kitchen & Bath Drawing

## LIST OF PHOTOS

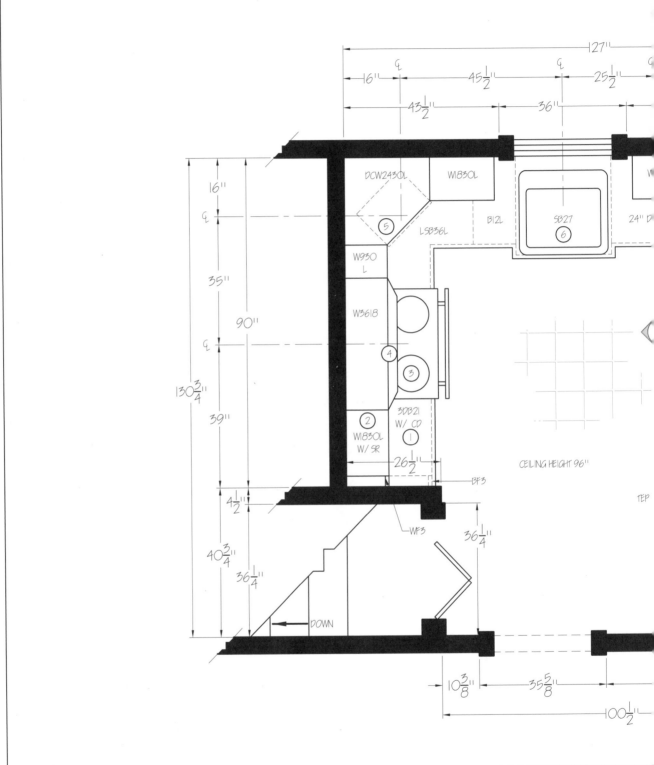

**NKBA** *The Finest Professionals in the Kitchen & Bath Industry*

National Kitchen & Bath Association℠

DESIGNED

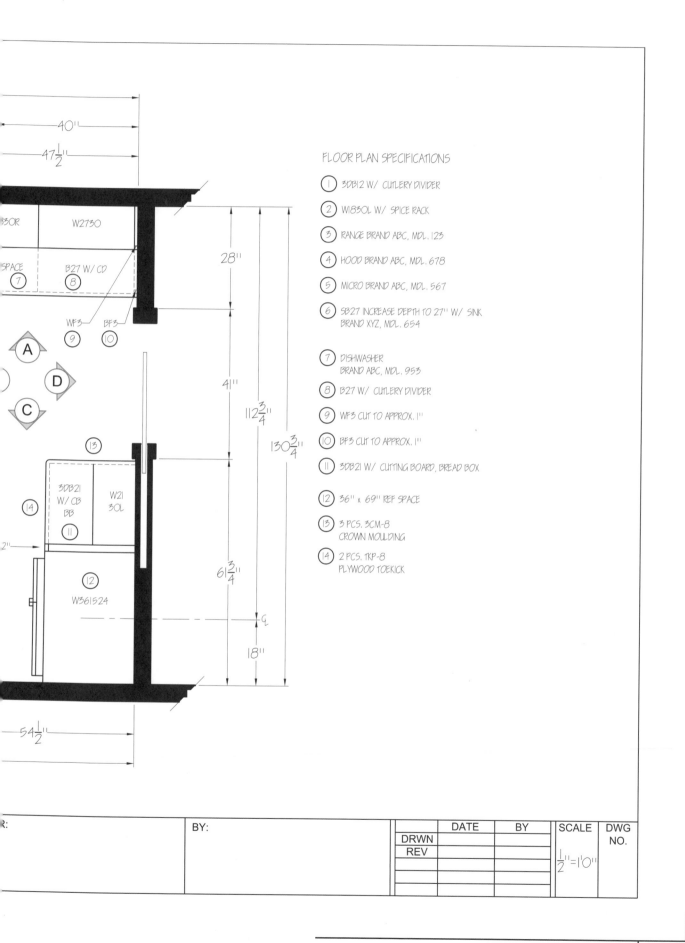

FLOOR PLAN SPECIFICATIONS

1. 3DB12 W/ CUTLERY DIVIDER
2. W1830L W/ SPICE RACK
3. RANGE BRAND ABC, MDL. 123
4. HOOD BRAND ABC, MDL. 678
5. MICRO BRAND ABC, MDL. 567
6. SB27 INCREASE DEPTH TO 27" W/ SINK BRAND XYZ, MDL. 654
7. DISHWASHER BRAND ABC, MDL. 953
8. B27 W/ CUTLERY DIVIDER
9. WF3 CUT TO APPROX. 1"
10. BF3 CUT TO APPROX. 1"
11. 3DB21 W/ CUTTING BOARD, BREAD BOX
12. 36" x 69" REF SPACE
13. 3 PCS. 3CM-8 CROWN MOULDING
14. 2 PCS. TKP-8 PLYWOOD TOEKICK

| | DATE | BY | SCALE | DWG NO. |
|---|---|---|---|---|
| DRWN | | | $\frac{1}{2}"=1'0"$ | |
| REV | | | | |
| | | | | |
| | | | | |
| | | | | |

R:      BY:

# APPENDIX

## KITCHEN FLOOR PLAN

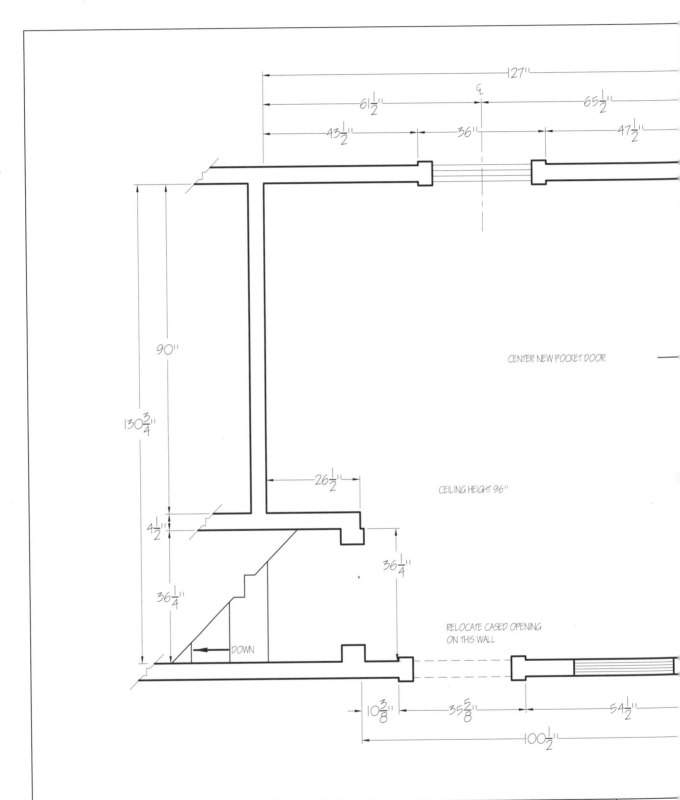

127"

61½"    ⊄    65½"

43½"    36"    47½"

90"

130¾"

CENTER NEW POCKET DOOR

CEILING HEIGHT 96"

26½"

4½"

36¼"

36¼"

RELOCATE CASED OPENING
ON THIS WALL

DOWN

10⅜"    35⅝"    54½"

100½"

**NKBA** *The Finest Professionals in the Kitchen & Bath Industry*
National Kitchen & Bath Association℠

DESIGNED

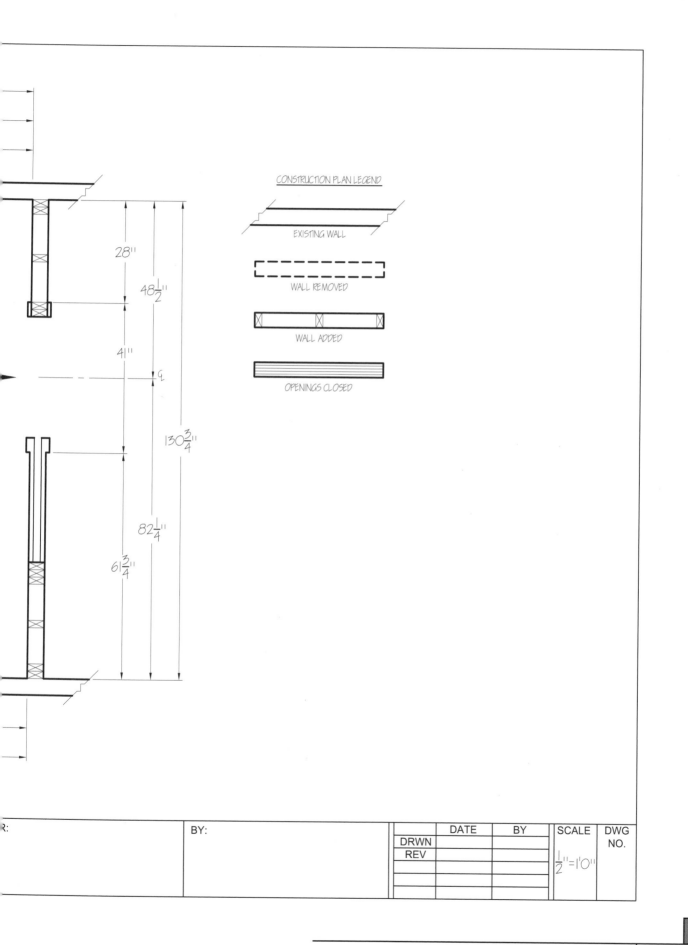

CONSTRUCTION PLAN LEGEND

EXISTING WALL

WALL REMOVED

WALL ADDED

OPENINGS CLOSED

28"

48$\frac{1}{2}$"

41"

$\mathsf{C}_L$

130$\frac{3}{4}$"

82$\frac{1}{4}$"

61$\frac{3}{4}$"

| | | DATE | BY | SCALE | DWG NO. |
|---|---|---|---|---|---|
| | DRWN | | | $\frac{1}{2}$"=1'0" | |
| | REV | | | | |
| | | | | | |
| | | | | | |
| | | | | | |

R:

BY:

# KITCHEN
# CONSTRUCTION PLAN

# KITCHEN
# MECHANICAL PLAN

## BATH FLOOR PLAN

# BATH
# CONSTRUCTION PLAN

# BATH
# MECHANICAL PLAN